# DO YOU KNOW I CRY DURING YOGA?

Letters From A Wife Who's Leaving

Wren Waters

Copyright © 2019 Wren
Waters All rights reserved

It's good to be loved but it's even better to be understood.

- Ellen DeGeneres

Dear Reader,

My marriage is unhappy.

Deeply, desperately, devastatingly unhappy.

I had no idea – *no idea* – one could be this unhappy in a marriage,

Even more shocking, more debilitating is that I had no idea one could be *this* affected by the unhappiness of an unhappy marriage.

My marriage is draining every last drop of life right out of my soul.

Wringing it completely dry.

And yet, for so very long – so, very, very, *very* long – it has crushed me to think of leaving.

Whatever the magnitude of my shock at finding myself so unhappily married is, it dwarfs in comparison to my shock at finding it so difficult to leave.

Who wouldn't just leave an unhappy marriage?

Why would anyone find it hard – I mean *really hard* - to leave an unhappy marriage?

Well, the truth is lots of women don't "just leave" an unhappy marriage because lots of women – like myself - find it surprisingly hard to leave an unhappy marriage.

The end of a marriage, I now realize, isn't something that happens once and is done.

The end of a marriage is something that follows you the rest of your life.

The end of raising children together.

The end of celebrating holidays and accomplishments together.

The end of the dreams and plans you made for your life together.

It's the end of your future as you envisioned it.

(And don't even get me started on having to check the "divorce" box on every form you ever fill out for the rest of your life! What is

THAT even about? The grocery store/Costco/vet's office needs to know your marital status – your marital failure - before issuing a membership/grocery savings card and/or giving Fluffy a rabies shot?)

No, ending an unhappy marriage, even when you feel the life draining out of your soul, is no easy or simple thing.

And yet, what can you do when you find yourself so tragically unhappy in your marriage?

As the years of sadness, emptiness, regret and resentment for my marriage – for my entire life really - stretched on, I knew I couldn't stay and yet I couldn't get my head (or heart) around leaving.

The obvious question, the natural curiosity when someone talks about how unhappy she is in her marriage is,

"Why?"

"What's wrong?"

And of course, what that really means is,

"What's wrong with *him?*

At first thought, it seems a justified question.

A reasonable inquiry.

And I was more than willing and ready to lay it out here.

But interestingly, in preparing myself to leave, I realized I had to let go of identifying the why as it related to my husband. Oh, there are plenty of clues in these letters I've written. A reader will certainly get a clear picture of my marriage from my perspective. But ultimately, when you feel yourself dying at the hands of your marriage, saving yourself and resurrecting your life has nothing to do with the problems in the marriage or all the ways your husband is and/or has been wrong.

Don't misunderstand.

I spend years – *years!* - blaming my husband. And I say, almost un-apologetically, I believe with reasonably good and warranted cause.

But you know what?

If you're in a unhappy marriage.

If you fear your very being is dying.

One day the Why doesn't really matter.

One day you have to completely divorce yourself (no pun intended) from the Why as it pertains to your spouse.

What I have learned about the foundations of unhappy marriages is they are all simply different paths leading to the same destination. At the end of the day, no matter how your spouse got you there – the addiction path? The adultery trail? Depression, bipolar, mental health track? Abuse route?

It really doesn't matter.

Not that your pain and grief don't matter but ultimately, no matter the particulars, all the suffering and loneliness, the disappointment and anguish, the empty shell left where your soul once was, is universal for those of us in unhappy marriages.

Like soldiers dying in war, the exact cause may be different but the outcome is the same.

So what to do with this pain?

Me, I wanted out.

But I couldn't seem to process leaving before I left.

And I couldn't leave til I processed having to go.

How was I going to process the pain of leaving – so I could leave?

I decided to start writing letters to my husband.

He and I had progressed (digressed?) beyond even the most simple and basic of conversations. (There were more days than I care to count where we had literally not said more than ten words to one another.) And if you can't even talk about "how was your day at work today" or "the dog got out of the yard again," then honest, often difficult communication that leads to understanding, growth and intimacy has about the same chance as the proverbial snowball in hell. And if you can't talk about your runaway dog or your feelings about your marriage, sorry Gwyneth Paltrow, but you sure as heck ain't going to be working together on "conscious uncoupling" anytime soon. No, make that anytime *ever!*

So…

I was miserably unhappy in my marriage.

I was miserably unhappy in my life.

I couldn't talk *to* my husband.

I couldn't bring myself to *leave* my husband.

Yet, neither could I continue living the way we were living while remaining silent. There were things I needed to say. Things I needed him to hear. And I had to get my heart to align with what my head already knew was necessary.

It has been incredibly cathartic and healing to commit my pain, sadness and yes, even hope to paper.

I hope in reading these letters, you might find the way to your own cathartic awakening, your own hope and healing and, perhaps even, your own renewed passion for living.


Wren Waters
August 10, 2019

*If it comes, let it stay. If it goes, it's ok, let it go. Let things come and go. Stay calm, don't let anything disturb your peace, and carry on.*

*- Germany Kent*

January 16, 2018

Dear J.,

I am leaving you.

I don't know when and I don't know how but I know I have to.

Of course, it's not as though this is the first time these thoughts have occurred to me. The first time these emotions have risen up in me.

No, these feelings, these emotions, have been been continuously cresting and falling within me for a long time. A life at sea with the sea within.

Raging storms threatening to destroy me followed by the bluest skies, the calmest waters that threaten to fool me.

It's the emotional backdrop of my life these days.

Has been for a long time.

The desire, the need, the longing to leave.

The desperation to be gone.

Followed by.

Followed by what?

Hope?

Naivete?

Ambivalence?

Lethargy?

This has been my internal struggle for a long time now.

Too long.

I can't stay but I can't bring myself to leave either.

But now, now I am ready.

No, no I take that back.

No woman is ever ready.

But I am resolved.

I'm ready to be ready.
All this time I thought it was about me.
But it's not about me.
It never was.
I just didn't know it.
Until now.
It's about My Life.

These letters are to "forewarn" you in retrospect. (Is that even such a thing?) These letters are to explain to you what may come as a shock to you though I don't know why.

The truth is you left me a long time ago.

Not physically of course. In fact, your physical presence is about all that is left of you in the house. In our marriage.

You are emotionally and mentally gone. I am little more than a roommate to you and barely even that. I am certainly not a wife to you. I wish it didn't matter. I wish I could live a happy, passionate life while being your roommate. But I can't. You are like an anchor on my soul while I try to swim the sea of life.

You are here but you are gone.

How is it you have left and yet remain to weigh me down?

How can your absence be such a foreboding presence?

*Wherever you are, be there totally. If you find your here and now intolerable and it makes you unhappy, you have three options: remove yourself from the situation, change it or accept it totally. If you want to take responsibility for your life, you must choose one of these three options, and you must choose it now. Then accept the consequences.*

*- Eckhart Tolle*

January 17, 2018

Dear J.,

It would seem that leaving you should be an easy thing.
You are withdrawn.
Cut off.
Closed off.
Verbally abusive.
You are volatile, unpredictable, selfish and uninterested.
It should be a simple thing. Straight-forward, easy-peasy to leave you, right?
Turns out it is anything but.
Turns out leaving your husband, even one who is all the above, is an emotionally convoluted and complex thing. Like climbing a mountain trail with 100's of switchbacks.
I am continually moving forward in my emotional and mental effort to leave you only to double back around to thinking about staying with you.
I want to leave.
Oh I want to leave.
"WHEN THE HELL CAN I LEAVE?" My soul screams.
But then…
I don't want to leave.
Wanting to leave but not wanting to leave.
How am I suppose to decide?
When do I decide?
How many gut-wrenching, soul-sucking encounters or incidents or blow-ups does it take to convince me to the deepest core of my being that I need to leave?
I don't know.

But I think perhaps, when it is no longer about my *desire* to leave and it becomes about my *need* to leave…my resolve will be found. Clarity will present itself.

*The certainty we hunger for in human relationships is most poignantly unachievable when a person we care is about is neither clearly absent nor clearly present in our life.*

*- Pauline Boss*

January 18, 2018

Dear J.,

You anger me.
Your presence angers me.
Just your presence.
This is not a good place to be emotionally or mentally.
It pisses me off that I have to do things for you that you wouldn't do for me.
You are pathologically selfish.
What is yours, is YOURS.
When your car goes into the shop, I rearrange my life, my plans, my errands – my entire day - so that you can use my car. I call friends to ask for favors like picking up our kids. I reschedule and/or cancel things. I even WALK to where I want or need to go. All so that you can take my car to work. Which you might say,
"Well, I have to get to work…"
Of course.
Somehow your job, your responsibilities are more authentic, more valid, more important than mine.
When my car goes into the shop…
There is not even A DISCUSSION about how we can share the one (YOUR!) car.
"I want my car."
That's what you say.
Discussion over.
And yet it's the weekend.
You have no plans to go anywhere nor commitments.
It doesn't matter, you say. You want your car *JUST IN CASE YOU DECIDE* to go somewhere. (Never mind that you basically

NEVER spontaneously decide to "go somewhere."

This is not what I thought marriage would be.

I didn't have a lot of fairy-tale, happily-ever-after preconceived notions but I can tell you, I did expect my marriage to be a partnership.

And yet...

Would it surprise you if, (when) I said it still hurts me to think about leaving you?

It hurts to think of leaving you "behind."

I had an image flash in my head.

I am 60 years old, in a bar in Ireland though I don't know why or how Ireland popped into my head but it did.

Anyway, my random imagery not-withstanding, I'm in a bar in Ireland, well into this last "chapter" of my life and this stereotypical rogue of an Irishman with that accent that just melts women's hearts, falls in love with me.

I feel both happiness for my own life and sadness for you – my to-be ex-husband. I guess even standing in the rubble of our marriage's ruin – pain and disappointment, grief and resentment scattered at my feet – some love still remains.

*There are times when the actual experience of leaving something makes you wish desperately that you could stay, and then there are times when the leaving reminds you a hundred times over why exactly you had to leave in the first place.*

*- Shaun Niequist, Bittersweet, Thoughts on Change, Grace and Learning the Hard Way*

January 20, 2018

Dear J.,

Why isn't it easy for me to leave you?
Leave this dead marriage?
Why can't I just walk away?
Leave it lying there in the ditch for the vultures to pick at, the maggots to clean up.
But even a dead marriage was alive once.
And so when I plan on leaving, in my mind it's not the dead marriage I'm leaving.
I'm leaving the marriage that was once alive.
The marriage I thought would live forever.
The marriage I don't want to believe is dead.

*It's hard to leave – until you leave.*
*And then it's the easiest god damn thing in the world.*

*- John Green, Paper Towns*

January 21, 2018

Dear J.,

Why won't I say the words?

Verbally abusive.

I was telling someone I know about our situation – but only after she had revealed – unaware that my marriage and life mirrored hers - that she was in the same situation. She said,

"Yes, that's verbal abuse."

I felt myself tighten.

Become defensive.

Protective.

Of you!

I dance around the label.

To others as well as in my own head.

I say everything but.

I justify!

I hear myself saying things like,

"He doesn't...."

And then I fill in the blank with what you don't say and/or what you don't do.

But what about what you DO say?

Like calling me a "fucking bitch" or telling me to "shut the fuck up?"

What about when you are yelling – SCREAMING – about a broken refrigerator door or shoes left in the bathroom or the dogs barking? Or berating me for taking a piece of pepper as you cut up vegetables for stir-fry?

Yes, you yelled – SCREAMED – at me because I ate a piece of green pepper as you were making dinner. You probably don't remember. It was a long time ago. God, it was a long time ago. I can't remember the last time you were so engaged in daily life as to make dinner. Nonetheless, you probably wouldn't remember even had it just happened yesterday. You probably forgot your words as soon as they came out of your mouth.

But I remember. Not because I want to but because I can't help but to. How do you forget being verbally trounced upon in your own home? In front of your children? Because you ate a piece of pepper!

What about what you do Do?

Like violently throwing an object you deem "in your way?"

Stomping around.

Slamming doors.

I fear that the longer I live in this, the more I forget that this is not normal.

I know there are homes where no one is screaming because the dog barked or a towel was left on the bathroom floor or…

Someone ate a piece of pepper.

Ironically, there is also the flip side of your behavior that is as equally toxic and destructive.

You NOT speaking to me.

People often fail to realize that the "silent treatment" is very much a form of emotional abuse. You walk in the door and literally, do not say a single word to me.

Not so much as a grunt hello.

You spend the evening without any sort of verbal acknowledgment or engagement with me or the kids.

You go to bed without so much as a single "good night" to anyone.

Sometimes, in all seriousness, I think you talk to and engage with the dog more than you do with me or the kids.

Yes, this takes its toll too.

The silent treatment.
It's silent but it's not innocuous.

*Words may sting but silence is what breaks the heart.*

*The hardest part of being in an emotionally abusive relationship, it's actually admitting you're in one.*

*- Anna Akana,*
*So Much I Want To Tell You: Letters To My Little Sister*

January 23, 2018

Dear J.,

It's hard to think of leaving you.
So hard.
But soon, if I don't leave, there will be nothing left of me to leave with.
My soul is dying.
Withering on the vine of my life.
But who, what am I really leaving anyway?
You left me and our marriage long ago.
And yet, it's still not easy for me to go.
So when the day comes and I say it.
When I tell you I am leaving, do not make the mistake of believing my decision was "quick" or easy.
It's taking me ten years to "suddenly" leave you.

*You must make a decision that you are going to move on. It won't happen automatically. You will have to rise up and say, "I don't care how hard this is, I don't care how disappointed I am, I'm not going to let this get the best of me. I'm moving on with me life."*

*- Joel Osteen,*
*Your Best Life Now: 7 Steps To Living At Your Potential*

February 8, 2018

Dear J.,

I will not be your victim another minute longer.

You want me to be hurt; you need me to be hurt.

You want me to feel defeated because it keeps me here.

You need me here.

You say you don't want me here and that may be true but you need me here.

You need me here so that you have a place to dump all your anger, all your hostility, all your fear.

See I know.

Deep inside, I know.

I know all the viciousness, all the anger, all the hateful contempt and the ugly disdain you spew at me is really all the viciousness, all the anger, all the hateful contempt and ugly disdain that you carry within you, for yourself, that you can't bring yourself to face or handle.

I know that.

And perhaps that is why I feel bad to leave you.

But what can I do?

How long can I bear the weight of your demons?

*Objectification is a critical reason why an abuser tends to get worse over time. As his conscience adapts to one level of cruelty – or violence – he builds to the next. By depersonalizing his partner, the abuser protects himself from the natural emotions of guilt and empathy, so that he can sleep at night with a clear conscience. He distances himself so far from her humanity that her feelings no longer count, or simply cease to exist. These walls tend to grow over time, so that after a few years in a relationship, my clients can reach a point where they feel no more guilt over degrading or threatening their partners than you or I would feel angrily kicking a stone in the driveway.*

*- Lundy Bancroft, Why Does He Do That? Inside The Minds of Angry and Controlling Men*

February 10, 2018

Dear J.,

> I don't want to leave.
> Really!
> I..
> Don't...
> WANT to leave.
> I don't know if I will ever *want* to leave.
> But what can I do?
> I need to leave.
> I must leave.
> To stay is to watch you...
> Our marriage...
> Time...
> Even the inertia of my own indecision,
> Erode the essence of my very being.
> To stay is to lose even more of what I have already lost.
> To stay is to choose you over my life.

*The only thing more unthinkable than leaving was staying;*
*the only thing more impossible than staying was leaving.*

- Elizabeth Gilbert, Eat, Pray, Love

February 18, 2018

Dear J.,

I'm not trying anymore.

I know you won't understand this.

I know you feel I never try. That's what you always say when I beg you to try.

"YOU DON'T TRY!" It's clearly an accusation.

But I do (did) try.

Every day.

I get sucked in by whatever small kindness you extend to me but the next thing I know…

A sucker punch to the gut.

You're screaming.

Fucking this and fucking that.

No more.

I will not ever again believe that there is a chance, for you, for me, for us.

I will not ever again hope.

I accept it is over.

This may not be my first, second or even third choice but it is the choice I have to make.

I will not be angry.

I will be resigned.

*If you want to fly, you need to leave Earth. If you want to move forward, you need to let go of the past that drags you down.*

*- Amit Ray*

February 19, 2018

Dear J.,

Tonight I decided to write a letter to our marriage. I thought it might help me solidify things in my head and my heart.

Dear Marriage,

I am sorry but it is over.
I have to go.
More to the point, I have to let YOU go.
Good-bye.
I'm sorry.
I really, really am.
It's not what I want but it's what I need.
I'm sorry.
So very, very sorry.
Good-bye.
Love,

*It's hard to give up on being with someone.*

*- Lois Lowry, A Summer To Die*

February 20, 2018

Dear J.,

You have made you choice and it is clear it is not me or our marriage. I am under no illusion that I am perfect but your verbal abuse and outbursts are not acceptable or excusable or justifiable. We many not be physically separated but emotionally, mentally and spiritually we are already divorced. What is there between us? You leave in the morning without saying "good-bye;" you come home at night and don't utter so much as a "hello." I wish you could understand how much this nothingness affects me. I wish you could know or would acknowledge or open yourself up to appreciating that your empty presence is not innocuous. Your silence is not painless. Your lack of participation is not harmless.

Far from it.

Worse really.

It is a cancer.

A tumor of resentment growing in me.

I don't know how your behavior – or lack of behavior I should say- can't not be "on purpose."

I don't know how you aren't trying to be so hurtful.

I don't remember when you stopped kissing me good-bye all together in the morning

I'm sure you were mad about something one morning and so didn't kiss me good-bye.

And then didn't another morning.

And then another.

Until now.

These things matter.

Little rituals.

That keep you connected.
Even in the unhappy times.
Especially in the unhappy times.
First the lack of a kiss good-bye is representative of a problem; then it becomes the problem; then it creates more problems.
It's the slow dripping water carving a canyon in the rock.
How can anything be left between us?
If you won't even kiss me good-bye?

*Being alone is scary but not as scary as feeling alone in a relationship.*

*- Amelia Earhart*

February 21, 2018

Dear J.,

It's sad living with you here.

So sad that sometimes that sadness seeps into my soul and comes out as anger.

Anger at the kids.

The dog.

The house.

The laundry.

The dishes.

My own life.

Just sad, destructive anger.

I don't want to be sad anymore.

I really don't want to be angry anymore.

Yesterday I got mad – SO MAD – because the woman at the gas station wouldn't pull up so I could reach a pump. I had to wait until she pumped her gas and left.

I was seething!

And I thought,

"This is what J. must feel like all the time."

This disproportionate anger to a relatively harmless, pointless event or situation.

I don't want to be sad anymore.

I really don't want to be angry anymore.

It's about control, isn't it?

Your anger erupts when you feel out of control.

I see that now in my own anger.

The dog barking – can't control it.

The kitchen you and the kids leave a mess – can't control you or the kids.

The laundry and house and everything else that I can't control… anger.

It is eating me from the inside out, isn't it?

Poisoning me and then going on to poison those around me.

I can't do this anymore.

I have to find a way.

To not be sad.

Not be angry.

It breaks my heart to see you giving away the days of your life to this anger.


But it will absolutely crush my heart if I allow myself to lose the days of my life to this anger.

Your anger.

That is becoming mine.


*Anger is a manifestation of a deeper issue…and that, for me, is based on insecurity, self-esteem and loneliness.*

*- Naomi Campbell*


*Anger is an acid that can do more harm to the vessel in which it is stored than to anything on which it is poured.*

*- Mark Twain*

February 24, 2018

Dear J.,

    This is what you should know:
I never hated you.
You say I do.
You think I do.
But I never hated you.
It would be so much easier if I did hate you.
Could hate you.
I'd walk away and never look back again.
Hate has firm lines.
An outline that is definite.
No, I loved you.
Love has blurry lines.
Lines that curve.
Lines that move.
    If I could just feel hate for you, completely and always, it would be so much simpler.
No, I do not hate you.
What I hate is what this marriage is doing to me.
Who it is turning me into.
I do hate that.
Firm and hard.
No ambivalence there.
I feel myself becoming an angry, hostile person.
    Sometimes it is like I am outside myself as I witness myself being mean. Harsh. Unkind. I see it happening but I seem unable to stop myself.
    What has happened to me?

I can't live this way.

I can't be this woman.

The end of our marriage is more painful than you will ever know.

More painful than I ever expected it would be.

But I can't continue to watch myself become a person I don't want to be.

*When you get married, you are actually marrying three people. The person you are marrying. The person you think you are marrying. And the person they become as a result of being married to you.*

February 27, 2018

Dear J.,

    Good-bye.
    I left today.
    I know you don't know it and I know you won't understand until much later but today is the day I mentally, emotionally and spiritually left you and our marriage. Next year I will leave physically.
    I'm sorry.
    I am.
    But I don't know how to reach you. I don't know how to get into where you are inside. How to get past all you have put up to keep me out.
    I don't know what you need to feel safe enough to open up to me.
    *I don't know who you need me to be.*
    Whoever it is, it's not who I am obviously.
    Is there something different I could do? Someone different I could be? Is it me?
    Or is it life?
    You are so angry. So hostile. I used to always know why you were mad, even if it didn't make sense to me or seemed an issue not to warrant your wrath, I at least knew why.
    But lately, I have found myself not even knowing why you are mad. You just are. I don't know what an anger like that does to a person but I do know what it does to the people around him.
    I am feeling hostile.
    With no real why.
    I am feeling angry.
    Beyond what a situation warrants.
    Today I commit myself to being gone – emotionally, spiritually, mentally.

Until I can be gone physically.
Good-bye.
I'm sorry.

*The same force that shuts others out shuts you in.*

*- Bill Copeland*

February 27, 2018

Dear J.,

This morning I said "good-bye" to you in a letter.

And yet tonight, I tried again to engage you. To break through whatever this fortress is you have erected around yourself. It is so cliched for me to talk about walls or fortress or not being able to get in but it's also so true, so applicable. It is maddening. It is nearly beyond my ability to comprehend how completely, with absolute resolute you have shut me out.

I wish I could be a better person.

I wish I could love the anger in you away.

I wish I could forgive you.

I wish I could be the person that makes you feel safe.

But I can't.

Maybe a better person, a better woman, a better wife could.

But there is a resentment too deep within you for me to permeate.

I wish you would purge yourself of it and let us try.

I wish you would just allow yourself to explode, (rather than continue to *implode* as you are doing now)burst wide open emotionally and allow all these toxins to gush out.

But it's clear those are my hopes and wishes, not yours. And indeed, your journey is your journey to make as you decide.

I will accept this is over.

*There's an important difference between giving up and letting go.*

*- Jessica Hatchigan*

February 27, 2018

Dear J.,

Tonight's letter is to the Beast I fear resides in you. Has taken over you.

Dear Beast,

Who are you?
Anger?
Alcoholism?
Depression?
Whoever you are, it is clear you have him firmly in your filthy talons. Razor sharp, they dig into his flesh.
You will not let him go.
You are determined to devour him.
He is resigned, apparently, to letting you do so.
You want me too.
I know that.
I feel the piercing sting of your claws as they slash at my soul too.
I see the haunting reflection of you in me when I look in the mirror.
I am aware that you would love nothing more than to take me as your prey as well.
I know too.
Feel…
See…
Sense.
That you have been succeeding.
That your claws have been sinking deeper, your fangs ripping off more and more pieces of my soul.

But it stops here.
You will not devour me.
You will not defeat me.
You will not take me with him.
I can't fight you for him.
But I will fight you for me.

*The wild, cruel beast is not behind the bars of the cage. He is in front of it.*

*- Axel Mumthe*

March 12, 2018

Dear J.,

I have said good bye to you so many times but never left.
Last night I left.
Maybe not physically but emotionally, mentally, spiritually, I left.
I can't stay another minute longer.
It is far, far harder for me to leave than you will EVER know.
It's nearly impossible for me to leave while I am still here.
But I have to find a way.
I have to find a way to be here but not be here.
You are apparently very good at it.

You come home every evening, you are home all week-end but you are most certainly not here. How do you do it? How do you mentally remove yourself from your physical presence?

*Do not hold your breath for anyone,*
*Do not wish your lung to be still,*
*It may delay the cracks from spreading,*
*But eventually they will.*
*Sometimes to keep yourself together*
*You must allow yourself to leave,*
*Even if breaking your own heart*
*Is what it takes to let your breath.*

Eric Hansen

March 15, 2018

Dear J.,

    The hardest thing I ever did is prepare to leave you. It's taken me five years of prep work just to be ready to prep! I don't know if you will ever know, ever believe, how hard it has been for me. It's been excruciating.

    It sickens me to think of being successful at leaving you, breaking up our family. Sickens me to think of us becoming intimate strangers; sickens me to imagine how we will come to move around one another in that awkward effort at civility whenever we attend one of the kid's events or see each other in passing. I hate the thought that our marriage will be deemed a "failure." Another statistic. I will forever bear the label of "divorced." Have to check off that box at the doctor's office, on insurance forms, motor vehicles. Library card? Do you have to identify yourself as "divorced" when you get a library card? What relevance does your marital status even have to anything you might be filling out a form for? I don't know but that will be a new label. My new label. *Divorced.*

    But what options do I have?

    Just because my driver's license doesn't say "divorced…" Just because the world at large sees us as still married… doesn't mean there is a marriage there. People say marriage is "just a piece of paper." Perhaps that's true. Perhaps all the love and commitment is there regardless. Should be there regardless.

    Well, the same can be said of divorce.

    It's just a "piece of paper" because the emptiness, the loneliness, the pain, the loss, the sadness – it's all there long before and irregardless of what the state recognizes. What the outside world sees. What a "piece of paper" says.

I've asked myself time and time again if I still love you?
Then I realized the answer to that question is irrelevant.
I no longer love – or even like – myself.
I no longer love – or even like – the way I am living my life.
I am scared and I am hungry.
Scared I will die in our dying marriage.
Hungry for life to be what I know it can be.

I am more sorry than you'll ever know but it has become either you and our marriage… or me.

*It is only through labor and painful effort, by grim energy and resolute courage, that we move onto better things.*

*- Theodore Roosevelt*

March 17, 2018

Dear J.,

Sometimes it's hard to talk to you as I prepare to leave. Everything sounds so normal between us but there is this resentment, a hostility within me that nags at me when I talk to you.

I want to pretend it's not so but I deeply, deeply resent what brought me to this place. How *you* brought me to this place.

It's the way you speak to me.

I don't know if I can ever forgive you for the words you've hurled at me again and again.

"FUCK YOU."

"SHUT THE FUCK UP."

"YOU'RE A FUCKING BITCH!"

I don't even want to write the words here.

Words no wife should ever hear from her husband but more.

Words no child should ever hear their father say to their mother.

I know you don't "mean" them.

I know they are a product of your own pain and anger.

I know…

They probably haunt you as much as they haunt me.

Or do they just become more of the emotions you deny?

The pain that is feeding your inferno of anger?

I don't know.

It's not for me to know.

I have to remind myself we all have our own journeys in this one big journey called Life. I can't protect you from you.

I can barely protect myself from me.

*The world breaks everyone, and afterward, some are strong at the broken places.*

*- Ernest Hemingway*

March 23, 2018

Dear J.,

I don't know if I'll ever show you these letters.
I want to.
It's why I am writing them.
I really want you to know the process I went through to leave you. The long, painful and difficult journey it was for me to get from being "us" to becoming just me. The other day when we were arguing – again – about money. It's always about money. I said,
"I know it's your money."
And you replied,
"It IS MY money!"
And with those words of yours, I think I finally got it.
I have wondered for a long time now how it is that you seem to have such complete and utter disdain for me. How it is you seem to loath me from the very core of your being. I've spent much time trying to get my head around the contempt you seem to hold in your soul for me, your wife, the mother of your children but now I understand:
You do not see me as your wife or the mother of your children or even a partner.
You do not see me as someone you are sharing your life with.
You certainly don't see me as your equal.
You see me as simply a taker.
A financial drain.
Someone (something?) that is costing you money.
*YOUR* money!
I have no value to you as your wife.
I have no value to you as the mother of your children.

In your eyes, there is nothing I bring to you, our children, our home, our life together.

In your eyes, I am hardly more than a freeloader.

No wonder you hate me.

*Anyone can give up; it's the easiest thing in the world to do.
But to hold it together when everyone would expect you to fall apart, now that is true strength.*

*- Chris Bradford*

March 28, 2018

Dear Marriage,

>Do you know how long I have clung to you?
>The illusion of you.
>The hope of you.
>I have clung hopelessly to the idea that you can be a happy, healthy, rewarding marriage that lifts me up. A relationship of mutual respect and love. A marriage of camaraderie and support. A marriage that is all the word "marriage" implies.
>I have clung SO LONG to that ideal of you but you, my marriage, are not that ideal.
>And you never will be.
>You are an anvil around my ankle while I try to swim, frolic and bask in the sea of life.
>I am declaring you, my marriage, dead to me.
>Do I hate you?
>No.
>Not anymore.
>I hated you for so long.
>I hated you for all you were.
>And all you were not.
>But I have forgiven you now.
>And let you go.
>It wasn't easy and I don't know that it will be easy – the process – but I have to let you go. You're never going to give me what I long for or what I dream of.
>And clinging to what I wish you had been only robs me of what can be. What my life can be.

*Letting go means to come to the realization that some people are a part of your history, but not a part of your destiny.*

*- Steve Maraboli*

March 31, 2018

Dear J.,

We talked last night.
More openly than in a long time.
But I still felt you were closed off from me.
I don't know that I want to "repair" anything.
You seem to be so acutely aware of all I have done to you, all the ways I have wronged you and yet, you seem to have no idea – or make any acknowledgment – of all you have done to me. The hurts I felt (feel?) from your actions.
You said I act like the world revolves around me.
That would make me laugh if it wasn't so tragic.
How you could ever accuse me of *that*, I will never understand.
I give my heart and soul and time to our children.
My every waking moment is about trying to give them what they need – emotionally, mentally, physically.
You go to work, come home, play video games and then go to bed.
You're checked out.
From me.
The kids, the house, our life.
I don't know how it seems to you that I am the self-absorbed one.
Even if you don't feel self-absorbed.
Even if you don't see how your actions look to me.
Even if your perspective on your behavior is 180 degrees from mine.
How…
How, how, how, how…HOW?
Could you even accuse me of being self-absorbed?
I wish you at least saw value in me as a mother to our children.

*If you didn't love him, this never would have happened. But you did. And accepting that love and everything that followed is part of letting go.*

*- Sarah Dessen*

April 3, 2018

Dear J.,

You will never, ever, ever know how hard it was for me.
You will never, ever, ever realize how the thought of hurting you hurt me. Kept me stuck. Kept me hurting me.
Every snippet of conversation from you;
Every remotely affectionate gesture;
Every small effort from you kept me hoping.
Holding on.
Wanting.
Waiting.
I didn't want to think of the day we were "ex's."
I didn't want to think of the day when we would be those awkward "strangers" standing next to each other at our kids' events.
I didn't want to "split" holidays or weekends or send my kids to "their father's" every Wednesday night.
I wanted to hold on.
To you.
To our marriage.
But holding onto you was killing me.
Holding onto our marriage was letting my life slip through my fingers.
I'm sorry you will never know…
How hard.
How painful.
How regretful it is for me.
To let go.
To end our marriage.

*The truth was, he now belonged only to my past, and it was time I begin to accept it, as much as it hurt to do so.*

*- Tammara Webber*

April 13, 2018

Dear J.,

Today I am writing a letter to this journal I am writing in.
I imagine that will seem rather odd to you.
I suppose that is fair.
It's just this journal is so pretty. The cover has a lovely drawing of a tree with its branches curving and curling every which way, giving the sense the tree is indeed alive. Full of hope. Full of potential.
That's what every new notebook or journal I buy represents to me anyway: potential and hope. Like somehow the blank, inanimate pages of a notebook can wipe clean all that plaques me, haunts me, weighs me down in my life.
The paper is quite nice as well. Creamy and delicious. Easy to write on, my pen gliding so easily even though the words are so difficult.
Is there a name for people who love paper, love pens, love the feel of pen across paper? Seems there should be. A word or term from medieval times when not just composing words but the physical act of writing was seen as an art.

Dear Pretty Little Journal,

I feel a little bad that you, with your lovely cover and creamy pages, have been assigned to hold the words, the feelings, the pain of a marriage ending. I hope you won't think of it as only recording pain; I hope you can see it as recording a metamorphosis as complex and complete as caterpillar to butterfly.

It seems so simple – the caterpillar spins herself a fluffy cocoon and weeks later, she emerges. Pops out – seemingly effortlessly – a new, beautifully winged creature.

But what if there is pain in the cocoon?

How can we be sure the caterpillar doesn't experience grief?

Trepidation.

Doubt.

What if she is trembling with fear as she spins her encasement?

What if she mourns leaving the life she is leaving, no matter the wonderment of the life she is going to?

What if she doesn't WANT to be a butterfly?

What if she begs the gods to leave her the little brown crawling creature she is?

Maybe it's harder for the caterpillar than we know.

Thank you, pretty journal, for being my cocoon.

For keeping me safe as I embark on my own metamorphosis.

*As with the butterfly, adversity is necessary to build character in people.*

*- Joseph B. Wirthlin*

April 14, 2018

Dear J.,

Thank you!
Thank!
You!

I am sorry for your pain but your pain, your sadness, your despair was the pain, the sadness, the despair that I needed. It was the pressure necessary for me to turn my hunk-of-coal life into a diamond!

I don't mean to sound as if I am happy or grateful that you are struggling and in pain. And I don't know why we came into each other's lives but I do see now that this marriage is allowing (forcing?) me to grow to my fullest potential in a way that a healthy marriage may not have.

Would I have preferred a healthy marriage?

Would I have preferred a relationship that allowed me to grow due to mutual respect, admiration, support and camaraderie?

Do I sometimes (Ever? Always?) wish we were one of "those couples" who took life on together and created a wonderful, fantastical adventure of a life together for ourselves? Our children?

Well, yes.

Of course yes.

A hundred times YES.

How could the answer to that be anything but "yes?!"

But…

But that's not how things turned out.

So what is my alternative?

The storm makes the mighty oak.

Thank you for being my storm.

*Every flower must grow through dirt.*

*- Proverb*

April 19, 2018

Dear J.,

I have been angry for so long.
I have allowed resentment to seep into the core of my being.
I feel a rage for you, for our marriage, for the entire situation engulfing me.
I can't live like this.
Indeed, there is a real physical danger to one's health. The human body does not do well living with such anger and bitterness, rage and resentment.
And so, with all I am, I will try to replace anger with love.
Resentment with gratitude.
Remorse and regret and sorrow with peace and acceptance and hope.
Thank you for coming into my life.
It it true I want more, I need more from a partner but thank you for what you can and did give. It is so hard for me to let go of the anger, the resentment but slowly I am emptying this bucket and refilling it with peace, gratitude, joy.

I am sadden our marriage wasn't "more."
I am disappointed it won't be the happily-ever-after we both wanted. Imagined. Expected.
But I will work to find the peace.
To be at peace.
It's the only way I can let go.
We think anger and resentment releases us.
We think if we keep the bitterness and rage fresh and accessible, we will change. Move on. Let go of the very thing, situation, person that is causing it all.

Nothing could be further from the truth or more self-destructive.

Love releases.

Peace moves us on.

Gratitude has the power to change us. Our lives.

It's taken me a long time to figure this out but I am (slowly!) getting it.

*Sometimes good things fall apart so better things can fall together.*

*- Marilyn Monroe*

April 22, 2018

Dear J.,

To me, it seems that you feel the need to be angry, hostile, resentful and fearful of life.
I see now (finally? Finally.) this is your journey to take.
This is not the journey I choose for me, for my life.
I love life.
I embrace life.
I believe in the abundance of the Universe.
I trust my dreams are meant to come true.
I have faith in myself and my ability to make those dreams come true.
I do.
I really, really do.
But that faith, that trust – in myself and in life – is being eroded by your anger, your fear, your doubt.
Do I "blame" you?
I can't blame you, I know that.
I have to take ownership, responsibility, blah, blah, blah.
We are responsible for our own happiness and all that jazz.
I know that.
But marriage is a partnership.
The ultimate three-legged race.
There is no way for one partner not to affect the other.
You either carry each other to victory…
Or knock each other down.
I can no longer allow my life to be tethered to your anger.
Your doubt.
Your fear.

I am ready to run.
I am ready to be free.
I am ready.
To live my life again.

*It takes courage to grow up and become who you really are.*

*- E.E. Cummings*

April 23, 2018

Dear J.,

I find myself thinking about and writing about your anger a lot.
A.
Lot.
Anger is such a powerful and corrosive force.
Especially when it is not your own anger!
I have allowed your anger into me.
My life.
I have allowed my soul to be corrupted by your anger.
I remember when we were new together.
I saw your anger then.
I said, "you are such an angry person."
You said, "so are you."
I said, "No. I may have a temper at times but I am not an angry person."
I could feel the difference.
But that difference is fading.
Eroding.
I am becoming as angry as you.
I cannot allow your anger to stay in my life a minute longer.
It's hard living with you.
So very, very, very hard!
Too hard as a matter of fact.
That's why I am buying my own house.
I want a house that is not a home filled with anger, hostility, yelling and cursing.
I want a house that is a home filled with laughter – loud, obnoxious, shaking the rafters, milk-coming-out-of-your-nose, laughter.

I want a house that is a home filled with warmth and joy and tranquility.

I want a house that is a home of safety – emotional, mental, spiritual – safety.

I want a house that is the home my children forever want to come to when they need to retreat from the world. The place that feels warm and safe when they are hurt or scared, anxious or lonely or just need a reprieve from the world-at-large.

A house where they know they can walk in the door, drop a bag of dirty laundry in the hallway and head straight to the kitchen for "free food."

Your anger permeates our home, it really does.

Its presence is palatable.

I feel the weight of its mass bear down on me the minute I walk in the door.

I feel your anger becoming my anger.

And that scares me a lot.

A.

Lot.

*You will not be punished for your anger,*
*you will be punished by your anger.*

*- Buddha*

May 12, 2018

Dear J.,

I don't know if you will ever know or appreciate the depth to which I thought about, worried about and grieved over our marriage.
I never *wanted* to leave.
But there came the day when I did *want* my life back.
There came the day I wanted *me* back.
It's not that my previous life was perfect.
It's not that I believed myself to be perfect.
But my life was happy.
I was happy.
I felt whole.
I was whole.
I was passionate and genuine and alive with life.
I liked me.
I liked life.
Now I am miserable.
My life is miserable.
Never, ever, EVER did I think I would consider my life "miserable." Never, ever, EVER did I imagine I would be muttering, hissing, screaming and/or sighing,
"I HATE my fucking life."
But I do.
I hate my life.
And I no longer feel whole.
I feel broken into a hundred little pieces.
Jagged shards of who I once was.
Fragments of the me I fully expected to be forever.
Littering my life like debris along the roadside.

Maybe you feel broken too.
Maybe you feel like a hundred jagged pieces too.
But I can't reach you.
I can't get in.
I tried to open up to you, to get you to open up to me but I failed on both accounts.
I tried.
Maybe you don't think I tried.
In deed, sometimes I wonder did I try "hard enough?"
Maybe you didn't recognize my efforts.
Maybe my efforts weren't what you needed.
But I did try.
Even if it doesn't seem like it to you.
Even if I failed.

*Probably one of the most private things in the world is an egg until it is broken.*

*- M.F.K. Fisher*

May 13, 2018

Dear J.,

It is 8:30 in the evening.

I am sitting at the dining room table eating a bowel of pasta with butter and salt.

Perfect Mother's Day "dinner."

Yes, today was Mother's Day.

I spent part of it hiding in the bathroom crying.

You did your part.

Or should I say, you did the minimum you felt you needed to do in order to fulfill any obligation you felt you had. You took the kids out, bought me some gifts, came home and presented them to me.

And then you retreated to the basement for the rest of the day.

Around 7 you came up, made yourself some "mini pizzas" and returned to your basement lair/hideaway.

It hurts.

Yes, of course it hurts.

All over Instagram and Facebook men are posting loving tributes to their wives. Telling the world how lucky they are, how lucky their children are to have this woman in their lives. Do our kids love me?

Of course they do. But what have you taught them about showing me respect and appreciation? What have you taught them about honoring their mother as their mother? Yes, if it sounds like I want to be put on a pedestal, the answer is yes, yes I do. As their mother, I do. Mothers give their all. They really do. Once a year, it's nice to have that celebrated.

In a big way.

With real effort.

Not just "phoned in."

*The most important thing a father can do for his children is love their mother.*

*- Theodore Hesburgh*

*Motherhood: All love begins and ends there.*

*- Robert Browning*

May 17, 2018

Dear J.,

    You'll never know who hard I tried, how much I endured, how long it took me to accept that our marriage would never work out.
    I know you think I believe everything is your fault.
    I do not.
    I do believe it is your fault we could not save our marriage.
    You withdrew.
    Quit.
    Shut me out.
    And when your silence didn't keep me far enough away, you yelled and cursed.
    Talking to you was like trying to talk to a badger as it shredded my flesh with its razor sharp claws.
    I probably will never convince you that I don't blame you for the problems between us.
    I don't blame you for the problems.
    I do blame you for not being willing to work together to change things between us.
    I do blame you for not being willing to work with me to save this thing called our marriage.
    But I am not angry.
    I do not hate you.
    I am simply ready to live my life to the fullest.
    Without the pain and the ugliness, the screaming and the silence.

*Negative emotions like loneliness, envy and guilt
have an important role to play in a happy life;
they're big, flashing signs that something needs to change.*

*- Gretchen Rubin*

September 4, 2018

Dear J.,

I am so angry at you.
So!
ANGRY!!
I feel like I hate you sometimes, I get so mad at you. You and this marriage have made my life hell! I'm mad at the kids. I hate the dogs. I hate this house. I hate everything you have done to me.
Yes!
I BLAME YOU!!
I blame you because you have given up on your own life, you have given up on this marriage, you've given up on us, you've given up on the kids and yes, you've given up on me.
You don't support me.
You don't believe in me.
You don't…
Love me?
I don't know.
I really, really don't know what you feel for me.
I know all the stuff you *spew* at me.
I know all your own shit that you project onto me.
I know the hatred you feel for yourself that you experience as hatred for me.
But I don't know what your true feelings for me are.
But then I guess you don't know yourself so how could I expect you to let me know.
It's not just you that I am mad about.
It's not just our marriage that you have trashed that I am mad about.

The house is hot as fucking hell!

We have no central air conditioning – don't even get me started on *that!!* And now the portable one we did have doesn't work correctly but you don't give a flying fuck! You're not the one cleaning up filthy dirty water from the damn thing leaking all over. You're not the one home all day in a hot house. (Yeah, that's one for the irritation books – the god damn thing leaks so I have to clean up the gross water but it doesn't even cool the house!) When you are home, you retreat to the bedroom where there is a working air conditioner. You won't buy one for the living area because, your words,

"Summer is almost over."

In other words,

"I don't care how miserable my wife and kids are. I'm not spending money on an air conditioner in September."

Then there is the dishwasher situation.

Yep, another broken thing.

Another thing you refuse to deal with (i.e. spend money on!) because hey, you're not washing dishes over and over again.

Nothing gets fixed or dealt with or addressed unless it affects *you*. And by "affects you," I mean costs you money.

I wish I could use my anger to my betterment. I wish I could take this seething rage and turn it into positive, productive energy.

Maybe I will one day.

Every morning I tell myself I will make this day that one day.

One day that will be true.

*I really believe that all of us have a lot of darkness in our souls.
Anger, rage, sadness, fear.
I don't think that's only reserved for people who have horrible upbringings.
I think it really exists and is part of the human condition.
I think in the course of your life you figure out ways to deal with that.*

*- Kevin Bacon*

September 5, 2018

Dear J.,

Everything about your behavior, your attitude and the way you speak to me says you don't want to be here.
You loath me.
I know it's not me you loath.
I know there is an anger feeding that loathing that has nothing to do with me.
But I bear the cross.
Of your misplaced wrath.
I stand witness to it and take the blows.
"SHUT YOU'RE FUCKING MOUTH!"
"YOU'RE A FUCKING BITCH!"
"I FUCKING HATE YOU!"
I'm not being a martyr or claiming victim-hood but how long can one human being bear such hatred, such ugliness, such toxicity spewed at her by another human being? Worse yet, it's the one human being on the planet who is most certainly *not* suppose to be spewing such hatred and ugliness and toxicity at her.
You go to work.
Come home.
Watch television and/or get on your laptop.
Play video games.
Then go to bed.
All this without so much as a "hello, I'm home" or a kiss good night or any conversation during the evening.
And it's not just me you ignore, shut out, seem to deny my very presence.
You treat our children the same way.

These precious, fleeting days of our children's childhood, being squandered and lost to your anger.

Now my anger.

I wish I had left sooner.

It seemed too daunting, too sad, too traumatic for them but now, it seems, surely the divorce-two-households-dad-every-week-end would have been better than this.

*Don't spend time beating on a wall,
hoping it will transform into a door.*

*- Coco Chanel*

September 7, 2018

Dear J.,

I am sorry you are so angry.
I am sorry that you are sad and hurting.
I am sorry for all your pain.
But I will not live this way any longer.
I cannot live in your anger.
Your sadness.
Your pain.
I want to seize life!
I want to soar high above the clouds.
I want to drink life up in big, sloppy gulps!
It seems life scares you.
Haunts you.
Like a dark figure in the shadows.
That's not what life ever was for me.
I can't let it become that now.
I can't.
I won't.
To me, life was never a cloaked figure lurking in the shadows.
To me, life is (was?) the big open sky, blue with puffy white clouds.
I can't live in fear of life any longer.
I can't live in your pain a day more.

*Your mission: Be so busy loving your life that you have no time for hate, regret or fear.*

*- Karen Salmansohn*

September 8, 2018

Dear J.,

You left long ago.

While I agonize and anguish, strategize and plan, justify and accept my desire to leave, you just left.

Long ago.

Of course not physically.

THAT would have been far easier!

No, you are here physically and gone mentally, emotionally, spiritually.

I just want that on the record.

That you left a long time before me.

When I leave physically, when the house is empty, when the kids and I are gone…

I don't want to be portrayed as the "bad guy."

The one who broke up our family.

The bitch who abandoned you.

Whatever the world thinks it sees or wants to believe, you and I know…

You left a long time ago.

I just wish you had done it physically as well.

*Do not be afraid: our fate cannot be taken from us; it is a gift.*

- Dante Alighieri

September 10, 2018

Dear J.,

I know you are hurting.
In fact, you are probably in a pain far deeper than what I can even be aware of.
But I can't live like this.
Your pain is not just destroying you
It's destroying me too.
It's destroying all I once believed myself to be.
All I once loved in and about myself.
It's destroying all I thought was good in me and leaving a monster in its place.
I can't live this way any longer.
I can't.
I won't.
I want to go back.
Go back to who I was.
Go back to what I was.
Go back to when.
Maybe that is the problem.
Maybe that is why I can't seem to move forward.
I'm trying to go back.
That who and what and when is past.
Over.
Gone.
I have to go forward.
Create who I can become.
Not in spite of you and me but *because* of you and me.
Because of the part of our own journeys we took together.

*Find our what you're afraid of and go live there.*

*- Chuck Palahniuk*

September 17, 2018

Dear J.,

I try not to be hurt by you.
I try not to notice the many ways your actions scream,
"You're not a part of my life."
Yesterday you met me at our daughter's soccer game.
You had stopped at McDonald's on your way.
You didn't bring me anything.
You hadn't called to see if I wanted something.
You just showed up.
McDonald's bag in your hand.

I sat there, just watching you eat. You were oblivious to me, to how your actions looked and felt to me. You just enjoyed your food while you watched the game. Ignorance is bliss, I guess.

Then you saw me watching you.
You got an odd look in your eye, like it suddenly occurred to you.
You had finished your sandwich and most of the fries. You held the container out toward me and said,
"Want the rest of these?"
No, no I did not want the "rest of" your left over fries.
The offer was worse than not thinking of me at all.
An after thought.
Is that all I am to you?
Is that all this marriage is to you?
It's like you have locked yourself in the house.
And every once in awhile you stop to take notice of me knocking at the door.
I probably should have stopped knocking long ago.

*Letting go doesn't mean you don't care about someone anymore. It's just realizing that the only person you really have control over is yourself.*

*- Deborah Reber*

September 22, 2018

Dear J.,

    I think perhaps you will never know how hard it was for me to leave you. How long and violently the debate raged in my head. What is it in negotiations when there is no middle ground? When what one side wants is completely contradictory to the other side's desires? It's called something – I forget what – but it's when there is no hope of compromise because the desired outcomes of each side are mutually exclusive.

    Well, whatever the official term for that is, that is the battle that rages in my head.

Leave.

Or stay.

There is no compromise.

No middle ground.

No place to meet half way.

And there are no winners.

When I leave, my side will not have "won" while your side lost.

Not at first anyway.

But eventually.

I'm sorry to say, eventually I will be the winner.

Specifically, my soul will be the winner.

I'm sorry.

More sorry than you will ever know.

But I am dying in this marriage.

Our marriage is killing me.

I want things from you that you can't, or won't, give me.

I didn't know how to extract from you what I needed.

I didn't know how to reach you.

You closed yourself off from me.
I am so mad.
So hurt.
But I am finally realizing...
You haven't just closed yourself off from me.
You've closed yourself off from everyone, everything.
Me.
The kids.
Yourself.
Life.
*I don't think you even has access to your own emotions as this point.*
I will worry for you.
I will grieve for you.
But I won't stay for you.
I can't.
I have to go.

*It always gets worse before it can get better. But it will get better. Like everything else, and like our past struggles, at some point we win, but before that win, there's always that loss that spurs us on.*

*- Dolores Huerta*

September 24, 2018

Dear J.,

Sometimes I'm mad.
Sometimes I'm sad.
All the time I am working on my resolved.
It's not easy to leave you.
Physically.
Financially.
Emotionally.
But there is nothing left between us.
I am dying.
The nothingness is killing me.
I just can't stay.

*When people divorce, it's always such a tragedy.*
*At the same time, if people stay together, it can be even worse.*

*- Monica Bellucci*

September 26, 2018

Dear J.,

Some husbands take but they do not give.

They allow their wives to give and give of themselves to them but they never reciprocate. They have shut themselves off from their own human need to give.

Yes, humans do have the need to give as much (maybe more?) as they need to receive but there are people, husbands, who close themselves off to that need. They simply take. And take and take and take. It may not seem as if that is closed off, as if that is distancing, but it is. We receive much in giving and to deny or refuse the human need to give is distancing. It is closing yourself off.

But you, my husband, have taken the art of closing off to an even deeper, more profound level. It is true you don't give much to me in the "random acts of kindness" sense. I miss that. I do. I wish I had someone in my life - my husband to be exact - that just did stuff *for* me. Isn't that the "point" of marriage: to make life's burdens – even the mundane ones – lighter?

But it's not just that you don't give.

You do not allow yourself to be *given to* either!

You have shut yourself off to such a depth that you also do not allow anyone – i.e. me – to give *to you*.

You never ask for help.

You won't accept any offers of help.

You won't allow yourself to need me or feel the slightest bit vulnerable to me. It really is an "advanced" tactic for someone who wants to close themselves off from the rest of the world. A maneuver that is hard for anyone not experiencing it to understand.

"How," I could imagine someone asking, even you asking, "can you be mad he won't ask you for help or let you do things for him?"

I can be mad, and even sad because it really is a way of disconnecting from other people. From the marriage.

It's not even as though I want to give and give and give to you.

Anymore.

Maybe once.

Maybe there was the day I wanted us to both give and take of one another but not now.

Our marriage is too dead for that.

But I would like to help you – as the father of my children, as a fellow human being, as someone I once loved? – on occasion.

But you won't allow me to be close enough to help you in even the slightest or smallest of ways.

You have ensured all avenues and pathways of connection and intimacy between us are blocked.

Closed off.

*If your eyes can not cry, then your gut will. The head and heart may be in denial of your human needs, but the gut will always carry the wisdom of your needs met and unmet, and thusly respond.*

*- Martha Char Love, What's Behind Your Belly Button?*
*A Psychologoical Perspective of the Intelligence of*
*Human Nature and Gut Instinct*

September 29, 2018

Dear J.,

I keep wanting things from you.

Needing things from you.

I am slowly realizing (accepting?) my stress comes not so much from not receiving what I want/need from you but from my *expectations* of receiving what I want or need from you.

How do I turn off those expectations?

How do I stop expecting you to be mentally and emotionally present when you are physically present?

How do I stop expecting you to participate in family life while I am still living with you?

I guess, in the end, you could say that's why I am leaving.

Because I can't be both with you and expect nothing of you.

It's killing me.

I could never have appreciated the power and toxicity of nothingness were I not living it with you.

You go to work.

Come home.

Take a nap.

Watch television.

Play video games.

Go to bed.

Get up the next day and do it all again.

And in between the work and nap and tv and video games, there is nothing.

No communication.

No participation.

No connection.

It's rotting my soul.
I finally see that I have to leave.
Not *because* of you.
But *for* me.


*I used to hope that you'd bring me flowers. Now I plant my own.*

*- Rachel Wolchin*

October 13, 2018

Dear J.,

It's finally over.
Finally.
I have to make the decision sound and firm that I am leaving you. I sometimes wonder if it's what you have wanted all along. Are you purposely being so cold, so withdrawn, so closed off so that one day I will have no choice?
So that one day I will do the "dirty work?"
So that one day I will be the "bad guy?"
Or are you so hurt, so broken that you just *can't* be present?
Am I confusing "won't" for "can't?"
I don't know.
I really, really don't know.
I've never thought of you as a manipulative person and I still don't.
But the level and intensity with which you are so closed off, so removed, so checked out is astonishing. I find myself thinking, how can it not be "on purpose?" Calculated. With profound effort.
How do you *not talk* to your wife or your kids day after day after day?
I guess it really doesn't matter because I absolutely can't live like this any longer!
I will be 60 next year!
60!!!
I cannot, I will not go into the final chapter of my life as an angry, broken, hostile woman.
Joyless.
I can't.

I.
Just.
Can't.

> *And in the end, it's not the years in your life that count.*
> *It's the life in your years.*
>
> *- Abraham Lincoln*

October 14, 2018

Dear J.,

When does it stop?
When do we both say,
"I won't do this anymore to me. To you."
When do we look at each other and say,
"I once loved you too much to let this become your fate?"
Tonight you screamed at me,
"SHUT THE FUCK UP!"
And,
"SHUT YOUR FUCKING PIE HOLE!"
Shut the fuck up.
Shut your fucking pie hole.
Shut the fuck up.
Shut your fucking pie hole.
Shut the fuck up…
Shut your fucking pie hole..
Shut…
The fuck up.
Shut…
Your fucking pie hole.
Shut.
Fucking.
Shut.
Pie hole.
Fucking.
Fucking.
Fucking.
Over and over and over again.

The kids in their rooms.

Listening.

Hearing.

Absorbing.

I rarely talk to the kids about this behavior of yours.

But tonight I chose to.

Our son said,

"It doesn't affect me."

I was beyond hurt.

It doesn't *affect* him to hear his mother spoken to in that manner? I asked,

"It doesn't affect you that your father screams at your mother, 'shut the fuck up?'"

He said,

"Well, not on some deep level."

He said it's not like it was "scaring him" or "anything."

I said,

"Well it's affecting me on a deep level and it's scaring me that the father of my children and my husband speaks to me in this manner."

I don't know how you got to the place within yourself where it's ok to scream at your wife, the mother of your children, with such vulgarity.

When you act like this, I want out so desperately.

I wish you would help me dissolve this marriage,

I wish you would meet me with compassion and kindness while we end what can no longer continue.

"Conscientious uncoupling," is that what Gwnyth Paltrow called it?

She received a lot of backlash for that and yeah, I have to say it's such an elitist, Hollywood nonsecular thing to say.

*But…*

At this point in my life, our marriage, I could use some "conscientious uncoupling."

You won't be kind in our marriage and yet, you won't be kind in the effort (need?) to dissolve it.

You refuse because you say it's "me."

You say that you are "happy" and "fine" when I am not around.

You say all your anger is *because* of me. (Not projected *onto* me.)

But I know it's not true.

I do know that.

I will not be held culpable for your anger.

You are too angry, too hostile, too mean and cruel and volatile for it to be because *of* me or *my* fault.

But, if you believe this is true…

If you think all this toxicity and hostility in our marriage, in our home is because of me…

Why won't you come together with me and help me end it in as peacefully a manner as possible?

*When elephants fight, it's the grass that suffers.*

October 17, 2018

Dear J.,

This morning it almost seemed normal.
Our marriage.
You and me.
As you left for work at 5:30 am, you found me standing on a dining room chair in the living room hanging up Halloween decorations.
"Have you been up all night," you asked. It seemed there was true interest, loving concern in your voice.
"No," I said. "Just since about 4:30."
"Sleeping hurts my neck," I added, referring to the insanely painful pulled muscle I am experiencing right now.
"I overslept," you say. "My alarm didn't go off."
And then you walked out the door.
No kiss good-bye.
No "be careful up there" or "is that the broken chair?"
Not a "see you tonight," "I love you" or even, "I'll be home the usual time."
Nothing.
You just walked out the door.
And with that, like some scene in a tv show, the fantasy burst and I was instantly reminded. Instantly back to reality. Instantly in the real state of our marriage.
I thought about what you did say.
"My alarm didn't go off."
And I realized I have tuned myself out from your life, your needs. Was there the day – I'm sure there was – there must have been – when I would have notice the time and that you weren't up yet and that you should be up for work?

Was there a time in our lives when I would have gone to you, gently nudged you, saying,

It's 5 o'clock…"

Was that ever there between us?

It must have been, right?

There had to have been a time when we were connected, our marriage was normal. When I would have awaken you before you overslept. When you would have come to me before you walked out the door. Put your arms around me and gently pull me from the chair, into you. And I would have laughed and kissed your neck and threatened to make you "late for work."

There was that time, right?

There had to have been.

Just had to have been.

But I can't seem to remember when that was now.

*Today expect something good to happen to you
no matter what occurred yesterday.
Realize the past no longer holds you captive.
It can only continue to hurt you if you hold onto it.
Let the past go. A simply abundant world awaits.*

*- Sarah Ban Breathnach*

November 1, 2018

Dear J.,

My feelings for you, for this marriage, are on a constant roller coaster ride. There are days when I see your pain – the deep, deep pain I know is there in you – and I hurt for you. I really do.

But then that pain manifests itself in the most ugly, severe and toxic, hurtful ways that I then ache to be free of you, of this marriage.

Will you ever really know – believe – the agony it's been to ready myself to leave you? Will you ever really know – believe – the painful journey it's been to end this marriage?

*My* marriage.

Perhaps not.

Perhaps you'll never really believe it was beyond hard for me to leave you.

That's why these letters.

So when I do leave, you'll know I didn't just "walk away."

This exit of mine is a long, slow and painful journey. Two steps forward, one step. Climbing Mt. Everest on my hands and knees. Pain in every step. Agony in ever movement taking me forward, further away from what I thought would be my life.

I never wanted to be "ex's."

I never wanted to look at each other as someone we "used to know."

I never wanted to be a stranger to the one with whom I was once so intimate.

*Now you're just someone I used to know.*

*- Somebody I Used To Know by Gotye*

November 21, 2018

Dear J.,

My heart breaks…
My head throbs…
From what you and this marriage is doing to me.
I feel physically ill as I write this.
The holidays.
Time for family, love, togetherness.
Not our holidays.
The holidays for us are time for heightened anger, tension and hostility.
The degree to which you shut me out used to confound me.
But then this Thanksgiving week-end it all became clear to me.
You're not trying to shut me out.
You're trying to keep me stuck with you!
Do you like this toxic dance?
Or need this toxic dance?
Is this how you want to live?
Or need to live?
Will you die this way?
In an emotional desert with an oasis just steps away.
I don't know?
I don't know what your journey is to be but I know I can't let this be my journey. I can't lay thirsting for life with water in arm's reach.
I just can't.
And I can't die this way.
No.
No, no…no.
I just can't.

I can't take my last breath knowing my life could have been so much more.

I can't take my last breathing knowing I could have been so much more.

I can't face the end of my life wishing I had lived my life better.

More fully.

To its fullest potential.

These thoughts scare me.

More, I think, than it scares me to leave you.

*Somebody should tell us, right at the start of our lives, that we are dying. Then we might live life to the limit, every minute of every day. Do it! I say. Whatever you want to do, do it now. There are only so many tomorrows.*

*- Pope Paul VI*

November 28, 2018

Dear J.,

Why do I keep holding on?
What am I holding on to?
It's certainly not my marriage.
I thought it was my marriage.
For a long time, I thought I was holding onto my marriage.
And maybe I was.
Once.
But not now.
Not anymore.
Now I am holding onto nothing more than an illusion.
A mirage.
A reality that ceased to be long ago.
A dream that has long died.
We are not partners.
We are not living life together.
We are simply living life in the same physical space.
We are living together separately.
All that remains between us that is real is the physical space.
And yet…
With each little gesture of yours – no matter how small – my head (heart?) springs back to…
Thinking?
Believing?
Hoping?
And yet, this Thanksgiving weekend has made it so clear.
You are my husband in name only.
A legality recognized by the state.

But you are not my husband spiritually, emotionally, mentally and intimately.

I will really be leaving a stranger.

*Loneliness is never more cruel than when it is felt in close propinquity with someone who has ceased to communicate.*

*- Germaine Geer*

December 1, 2018

Dear J.,

    I think of my mom and what she lost when my dad died at the age of 52.
    32 years of marriage.
    My youngest sibling 20 years old.
    All their kids just about out on their own.
    The years they had loved through but had also worked through. Sweated and toiled – physically, financially, emotionally in order to get to that sweet spot in life when your kids are grown, your finances are secure and the days ahead are all yours!
    The days when all the dreaming of a cabin in the woods or the open road in a camper or the beach house on the coast are coming to fruition. When dreams of grandchildren "dance like sugarplums in their heads." Everything my mom envisioned and dreamed of and looked forward to for her and my dad…
    Taken from her.
    A loss that is endless.
    Grief lurking beneath the joy of seeing her children marry, grandchildren being born, life playing out in the beautiful ways she thought she'd share with her husband.
    She lost all that.
    Ironically, I have the same grief.
    I mourn the future that won't be.
    I have lost the same things.
    Just in a different way.

*We must be willing to let go of the life we had planned,
so as to have the life that is waiting for us.*

*- Joseph Campbell*

December 2, 2018

Dear J.,

I can't do this any more.

I don't know who you are but you're not the person I married.

With ever fiber of my being, I can say, I *never* imagined you becoming the person you are today. Treating me the way you treat me these days.

And I never imagined me becoming who I am today.

I am mean.

Angry.

Cruel.

Volatile, hostile.

Un-kind.

I never thought I'd be such an un-kind person.

I used to be fun.

Happy.

Passionate.

Spontaneous.

Kind.

Yes, kind.

I'm pretty sure I used to be a kind person.

And alive.

I used to be *alive*.

Now I fear I am like fruit dying on the vine.

All the sweet potential being lost.

To bitterness and spoil.

*To be lost is as legitimate a part of your process as being found.*

*- Alex Ebert*

December 6, 2018

Dear Anger,

You cannot have me today.
You had me yesterday.
And the yesterday before that and the yesterday before that.
Too many yesterdays.
So today, not today.
I won't concern myself with tomorrow but today…
Today you cannot have me.
I will not do your bidding.
I will not be your mouthpiece.
I will not allow you to harm those I love through me.
Today you don't get to use me to spew you vitriol, spread your poison, perpetuate your ugliness.
I live from a place of peace and calm.
I live from a place of kindness and patience.
I live from a place of acceptance.
I live from a place of allowance.
Allowing all the gifts life has for me, all the potential within me.
I live from a place of gratitude.
You, Anger, no longer have any control over me.
You have had it too long.
You have poisoned me, hurt me, damaged me.
You have led me to hurt those around me.
Those I love dearest.
Not today.
I will not do your dirty work today, Anger.
You cannot have me.
Not today.

*It is only when we silence the blaring sounds of our daily existence that we can finally hear the whispers of truth that life reveals to us, as it stands knocking on the doorsteps of our hearts.*

*- K. T. Jong*

December 9, 2018

Dear J.,

There are times it almost seems like we have a marriage.
Like you are available.
Like we have a connection.
Almost.
Sometimes.
These almost-sometimes used to fool me.
I used to believe that they were real.
And that they would last.
I used to think I could trust these almost-sometimes.
But I can't.
They are fleeting moments of normalcy in a marriage that is far from normal or healthy.
Everyday the weight of what our marriage isn't weighs on me.
Threatens me.
Erodes me.
Kills me just a little bit more.
Everyday I feel a grief.
An anger.
A regret.
Of what is.
What isn't.
What should be.
What shouldn't be.
What was.
What will never be again.

*When one door closes, another opens; but we often look so long and regretfully upon the closed door that we do not see the one which has opened for us.*

*- Alexander Graham Bell*

December 10, 2018

Dear J.,

Of all the things that hurt me about our marriage, what probably hurts me the most is the way you treat me in front of my children. Our children.
You don't treat me with any respect.
You see no value in what I do for our kids or for our family.
You don't honor my contributions as their mother.
It's all (ALL!) about money.
The only thing that has value to you is money.
And since I don't earn a significant amount of money, in your eyes, nothing I do has any real value.
You deny this with your words when I bring it up, but your actions betray you. Your actions whisper louder than any words you could scream.
There is much written about the ills of social media. And no doubt, we see a very small, tiny piece of other people's lives in their postings. And I know…I know, I know, I know… What you see on Facebook or Instagram is hardly always an authentic representation of someone's life. And yet…
I see all the "shout outs" on Mother's Day by husbands extolling the virtues of what their wives do for their children and their family. The "happy birthday" wishes from husbands declaring their wives the "best thing ever to happen to them" and the "greatest mother any child could have…" Etc.,etc.
All the kind words and proclamations about how their wives hold everyone together, create a loving home, are the center of all that is good and loving in their family.
Etc,. Etc., etc.

Blah, blah, blah, blah, blah.

You would never dare state anything like that on social media.

And that's ok.

Really.

I don't need a Instagram shout-out or Facebook tribute.

But your daily actions…

The occasional word "in person…"

The example you set for our children…

If any of that represented some respect. An appreciation. A demonstration of value in my role in our family.

That would be nice.

*Our mothers give us so many gifts. They give us the precious gift of life, of course, but they also leave treasured lessons that can guide us along our journeys even when they are no longer with us.*

*- Maria Shriver*

December 12, 2018

Dear J.,

    Is there anyway for me to explain the depth and contradiction of my feelings for you and my emotions for our marriage? Will you hear or understand the magnitude of the conflict I feel over leaving you?
    Last night I felt such a hatred for you.
    I seethed as I sat there watching you eat dinner and watch your television show. Dinner you had prepared for yourself. The show only you wanted to watch. You were oblivious to us around you. It was as if nothing and no one existed outside your food and that god damn television. A bomb could have dropped on us at that moment, blowing us all to bits and it seemed as if you would not have noticed. Zombies could have come and dragged us away, kicking and screaming and I don't think you would have realized.
    Of course I am being sarcastic. Facetious. But it's not about facts: it's about how I feel around you. What you project.
    You are in such a state of pure disconnect from all of us, it turns my anger to such hatred.
    And that is where the conflict arises.
    How do you hate the man you once vowed to love forever?
    How do you leave where you wish you could stay?
    How do you reconcile the contradiction of emotions that ending a marriage creates within you?

*I didn't exactly want to get divorced. I didn't exactly not want to…
By then my marriage had become like the trail in that moment when I
realized there was a bull in both directions. I simply made a leap of
faith and pushed on in the direction where I'd never been.*

*- Cheryl Strayed*

December 21, 2018

Dear J.,

Money!
I hate (HATE!!) how you make me feel about money.
I have a raging headache right now just *thinking about* talking to you about money when you get home. I can't even write about how you make me feel because you make me feel so bad.
You make me feel like a paid nanny watching your children.
You make me feel like the maid hired to clean your house.
You make me feel like a child asking her father for her allowance.
I hate you for this.
I do.
I hate you for making me feel worthless.
But maybe I should thank you.
Thank you for motivating me beyond this existence.
Motivating me to become my own person – financially as well as emotionally, spiritually, mentally.

*It's good to have money and the things money can buy, but it's good, too, to check up once in awhile and make sure you haven't lost the things money can't buy.*

- George Lorimer

*Wealth is the ability to fully experience life.*

- Henry David Thoreau

December 27, 2018

Dear J.,

More than you may ever know, I am sorry. I am sorry our marriage didn't work. I am sorry I will leave you. I am sorry that some how I couldn't find the way to you.

But I will not, cannot, live in your pain any longer. It is a beast that has consumed you and it now threatens to consume me, too.

No, it does not threaten to consume me.

It has already begun!

Devouring my soul.

Feasting on all I once loved and enjoyed and valued in myself.

Ripping to shreds the joy and passion and enthusiasm I once held for life. For my life.

The world awaits me.

My life awaits me!

I cannot live in the hopelessness, the anger, the resentment.

The regret.

I never wanted to stand next to you and be someone you "used to know." I never wanted to be strangers with one I was once so intimate.

But I have no choice.

It is you, it is our marriage or…

It is me, it is my life.

It has been harder than you would think for me to choose me, for me to choose my life but it's really the only choice I can make.

It's the choice I have to make.

*It is difficult to find happiness within oneself, but it's impossible to find it anywhere else.*

*- Arthur Schopenhauer*

December 29, 2018

Dear J.,

Thank you.

Thank you, thank you, thank you.

You have given me the determination, the focus, the need to create great things for my life. You have forced me to leave the comfort of the uncomfortable and build my own life.

*Make my own money!*

I used to resent the way you made me feel about money – "your money," as you actually said it once.

You said it.

Your money.

And when I called you on it, you didn't try to deny it or start back peddling in an effort to undo damage you didn't mean to do.

No, you said,

"That's right. It's MY money."

*Your…*

Money.

You work full time.

I leach off of you.

That is how you make me feel, what I believe you believe.

Every single day.

But today I realized what a *gift* this is!

Rather than resent you, I will be grateful for you because I now know, I will never, ever be dependent on someone else…

For *my* money.

*Above all be the heroine of your life, not the victim.*

*- Nora Ephron*

January 2, 2019

Dear J.,

I don't know if I am mad, sad or just resolved.

I am leaving.

That's no longer a question.

I wonder if you'll ever know how difficult it was for me to come to this decision.

*To be comfortable with this decision.*

It's been a long, emotionally convoluted journey but your sadness, your anger is too much for me. It's becoming my sadness. My anger.

I don't want it to become my children's.

How much of your anger, my anger, your sadness, my sadness have they already absorbed? Never did I see this for my children. Never did I see this for you and me. The end of a marriage is hard for many reasons, of course but perhaps saddest of all, is the beauty of what was is lost. We're so (tragically) far from where we started. Do our children remember ANYTHING of the laughter and joy? The Saturday hikes or Sunday drives? Do they hold any recollection of you taking me in your arms, kissing me while their little voices screeched,

"EWWWWWWW!"

Maybe that is within them somewhere but is it in their conscious memory? Can they recall at will us being loving and kind to one another? Or is it all yelling and silence? Do they actively remember only the tension and unhappiness?

God, this was never-ever-ever- EVER who I thought I'd be, what I thought my marriage would be or the home I thought I'd be giving my children.

*I am a divorced child, of divided, uncertain background. Within this division I – supposed fruit of their love – no longer exist. It happened nearly forty years ago, yet to me nothing is sadder than my parents' divorce.*

*- Sylvia Kristel, Undressing Emmanuelle: A Life Stripped Bare*

January 13, 2019

Dear J.,

I don't know if I have any more words for you.

For us.

What is there left to say?

You have shut yourself off from me so completely that we barely speak ten words to one another on any given day. It used to hurt me to think of leaving you but with each passing day, it hurts me less and less to leave.

And more and more to stay.

*It was a long time in the making, my divorce.*
*One day became less special than the one before, and pretty soon we ceased all conversation.*
*It's a sad day when you have nothing left to say.*

*- Ricki Lake*

January 20, 2019

Dear J.,

I almost walked up to you tonight in the kitchen to hug you.
I almost put my arms around you to say something like,
"Let's make this work."
Almost.
But I wouldn't allow myself.
I reminded myself of the things you have said to me.
The way you have treated me.
I reminded myself that you will again say those things to me.
You will treat me the same way.
Was I wrong?
Should I have allowed myself?
Forced myself to reach out to you? (Allowed myself to reach out to you?)
I don't know.
I just don't know.

*Time doesn't heal emotional pain, you need to learn how to let it go.*

*- Roy T. Bennett, The Light In The Heart*

January 25, 2019

Dear J.,

I think this has to be my last letter to you.

I think I need to terminate all aspects of our emotional relationship so that I can work on terminating our physical relationship.

What does it say about our marriage that the only way I feel intimate with and connected to you is a one-way letter writing effort on my part? What does it say that I feel I need to "end" this solo-letter writing? That the process of writing you letters (that you, as of yet, don't even read) feels more real than our actual relationship?

I started writing these letters as a way of working through the process of leaving you.

The process of ending a marriage I didn't really want to end.

I didn't want this for myself.

For my life.

For you.

For the kids.

For us.

I never wanted this for us.

But what can I do?

Everyday I feel your emotionally and mentally absence in contrast to your physical presence.

It erodes my sense of being more than I ever would have imagined possible.

You have already left the marriage and me.

Maybe not physically but in every other aspect.

You are gone.

So what else can I do?

But leave too?

*There ain't no way you can hold onto something that wants to go, you understand?*
*You can only love what you got while you got it.*

- Kate DiCamillo, Because of Winn Dixie

January 26, 2019

Dear J.,

Tonight I realized that all my fighting for this marriage meant I was fighting to be screamed at. I was fighting to be ignored. I was fighting to be taken for granted, discounted. I was fighting to be disappointed.
I was fighting to be hurt over and over and over again.
So I decided…
It's time I start fighting to let go.

*Life is a balance of holding on and letting go.*

*- Rumi*

*He who knows when he can fight and when he cannot, will be victorious.*

*- Sun Tzu*

January 27, 2019

Dear J.,

Are you hurting?
Are you in pain?
Of course you are in pain, right?
How could you not be?
But are you hurting from our marriage?
Are you in pain for the way we have come to be together?
Or is your pain of another world?
Another you?
And has it created the pain you feel with me, being married to me?
I don't know.
I honestly don't know.
(It seems I am writing that a lot - "I don't know." But it's true. There is so much I don't know about how you feel, what you think, what is happening within you.)

The degree to which you have shut me out, to which you have closed yourself off says to me it can't be "just" us.

The magnitude with which you project your pain onto me honestly astounds me. And says to me it can't be about me. It can't be pain that I have caused. It must be old pain. Old pain that has nothing to do with me but for which I am the target.

I do talk to a select few friends about our marriage but I know it is impossible for them to comprehend the extent to which you are gone from me, from our marriage.

It is hurting me far more than I would have ever expected to leave you, to end our marriage. I would have never imagined that it would be so hard to leave an unhappy marriage. The doubt and guilt? What sort of feelings are these?

And love?

Is there still love within me for you?

I don't know. I don't know but I do know I have no choice.

I simply have no choice.

Everyday I wither more.

Everyday I feel myself slipping further and further away from the me I once knew myself to be. The me I want to be.

Everyday it becomes less about you, less about our marriage and more about what is happening to me. What I am losing in me. What I am losing in life. I never knew nothingness could be so corrosive. I never imagined emotional absence and silence would be every bit as toxic as yelling and screaming.

Nothingness is not nothing.

Silence is not innocuous quiet.

It's very lonely being alone with someone.

*Pray that your loneliness may spur you into finding something to live for, great enough to die for.*

*- Hag Hammarskjold*

January 28, 2019

Dear J.,

    Last night you walked up to me, a searing rage in your eyes and you hissed,
    "I fucking HATE YOU!"
    I willed myself to "ignore" you.
    I willed myself not to react.
    Outwardly anyway.
    But inside, my body would not deny the assault.
    It reacted. A physiological response that is beyond my control. I instantly felt it in my guy – as surely had you actually punched me. My muscles tightened, on heightened awareness. Waiting for another attack? An anxiety raced through my veins. I felt like I was going to throw up and faint at the same time.
    You came so close to me.
    Inches from my face.
    Spewing your vitriol.
    "I fucking HATE YOU!"
    How do I process that mentally? Emotionally? My body knows how to process it physically but the rest...I don't know.
    How do I wrap my head around this is who my husband is?
    How do I make sense of it?
    And how do I heal from it?
    I can feel what this is doing to me emotionally but what is it doing to me physically? How is my body carrying, holding this toxicity.
    I worry about that.
    I do.

*I was a high-functioning depressive, seemingly pulled together and buttoned down.
But inside deep, I was numb and mute. Now on the other side of divorce, I know that was me fragmented and doing my best to cope. But my body knew.*

*- Liza Caldwell, SAS For Women Cofounder*

February 10, 2019

Dear J.,

What you said last night.
I hear it when I look at you.
I hear it when I lay down at bed at night.
I hear it randomly through out the day.
"I fucking HATE YOU!"

It's not as if that was the first time you said that to me. You've screamed it at me so many times over the last years that I would have thought myself immune to it.

But last night was different.
More deliberate.
Calculated.
With an intention that has not been there before.

You didn't want the kids to hear. (Though why that was a concern of yours last night, I don't know. It hasn't been in the past.)

So you held it until you could approach me.
Get so close to me.

It makes me think of how I read once that detectives know that when a murder victim has been stabbed, the victim knew her/his assailant. It's so personal, stabbing. The two – victim and murderer – have to literally be touching. Connected. Not like shooting someone from a distance with a gun. No. Stabbing is definitely personal.

And that's how this was.

All the times you've shouted those words from across the room, it was like being shot with a gun. It didn't feel good but it definitely was different. There was a disconnect between you, me and your words.

But last night was a verbal stabbing.
You got so close to me.
You leaned into me.
*You leaned into me!*
And then with a slow, calculated cadence, you hissed,
"I…
fucking…
HATE YOU."
Each word punctuated.
Every word delivered with its own dose of poison.
I want to hate you too.
I do.
I want to FUCKING HATE YOU since that's how you allow yourself to feel about me.
I want to fill myself with the same loathing and disdain for you that you seem to feel for me.
But I won't.
I won't allow myself that hatred, that ugliness, that poison.
Instead, I will remove myself from you.
I will make you nothing to me.
Not the object of my love but not the object of my hatred either.
I started making just my side of the bed this morning.
You probably think that is out of anger. Hatred.
No.
It's out of resolve.
Resolve to never again be in the position where you talk to me that way.
Resolve to create my own life.
Resolve to be free of you physically, emotionally, mentally…
Financially.

*A bridge can still be built, while the bitter waters are flowing beneath.*

*- Anthony Liccione*

February 11, 2019

Dear J.,

I read the letter I wrote yesterday.
The words stung me though they were words for you.
"I will make you nothing to me."
How sad.
Tragic.
Is that what ending a marriage requires?
That the one once closest to us becomes nothing?
I don't know.
I've never ended a marriage and I'm not doing that well ending this one.
This is hard.
Really, really hard.
The constant barrage of conflicting and paradoxical emotions.
Mutually exclusive emotions, one would think.
How do I not love but also not hate?
How do I leave where I thought I would always stay?
How do I extend you grace while keeping myself detached?
I remember when our son was born.
How much it HURT at first to nurse him.
I wondered,
"Why doesn't anyone ever talk about this?"
How was it I knew so well the pain of labor and childbirth but never once heard so much a whisper about the (initial) pain of breastfeeding?
Divorce is like that.
No one talks about how really deeply difficult it is.
Oh, everyone says things.

"Divorce is hard."

"Divorce is expensive!"

"It takes time to get over a divorce."

Blah, blah, blah, blah, blah.

But no one seems to really acknowledge the years of pain and anguish and conflict – and I mean just within yourself!

*There's no pain or failure like going through a divorce.*

*- Jennifer Lopez*

February 12, 2019

Dear J.,

You are a mean man.

I know you are hurting.

I know there is pain and anger within you that runs deep and raging. Potent.

But that doesn't absolve you of responsibility for your actions. You have given yourself permission to say the most heinous and horrific of things to me.

And yet, I feel guilt at leaving you.

Why?

Why would I feel guilty at all?

I feel trepidation at leaving you.

Why would I feel trepidation at ending such a toxic relationship?

This guilt, this trepidation has presented itself as doubt for all this time.

Has manifested itself as procrastination.

I will will myself not to feel it.

I will will myself to not allow the guilt, the trepidation, the doubt to stall, delay or stop me.

I will will myself to remember leaving is not something I am doing *to* you.

It is something I am doing *for* me.

*To let go is to release the images and emotions, the grudges and fears, the clinging and disappointments of the past that bind our spirit.*

*- Jack Kornfield*

February 14, 2019

Dear J.,

Valentine's Day.
Cheesy?
Maybe.
Manufactured?
Aren't all holidays?
Isn't civilization by design "manufactured?"
But I digress.
Valentine's Day.
I include candy for you when I buy candy for the kids because why wouldn't I? I don't want the kids to see the divide between us. Who am I kidding? Of course they see it. I guess I should say I don't want the kids to see the divide between us 100%. I don't want them to think I am petty or unkind.
So I give you Valentine candy.
I know you won't give me any.
I tell myself that's "ok."
I tell myself I am not doing it "for you" anyway.
I am doing it for our kids.
So they don't see a pettiness.
Does it register in them that I give you candy but you do not give me candy or flowers or a little gift?
Do they think of their father taking but not giving?
What does this tell them about their parents' marriage?
About marriage in general?
About the roles of husbands and wives?
Or is this just "how it is" to them?
Do they not even notice?

Either way, it hurts.
On so many levels.
This absence of yours.


*Accustom yourself continually to make many acts of love, for they enkindle and melt the soul.*

*- Saint Teresa of Avila*

February 19, 2019

Dear J.,

I won't say you ruined my life.
But you certainly changed its trajectory.
And robbed me of a lot of opportunities I wish we could have pursued as a couple and as a family.
When we dated, it seemed you wanted to dream.
When we married, it seemed you could dream.
All the typical dreams but still unique dreams.
Our dreams.
Dreams of living a life beyond the ordinary.
Dreams of creativity and adventure and a life lived in and with passion.
But then something happened.
And over the years, every fantastical idea or adventurous dream I mentioned, you met with,
"We don't have the money for that."
Or,
"Where do you think we'd get the money for that."
Or worse of all,
No words.
Just a shrug at the absurdity of what I dared say out loud.
When did this happen?
Or did it not "happen?"
Was it there all the time?
Were you never the dreamer I thought you were?
Were we never synchronized in our approach to live?
Our lives?
I don't really believe this.

We were genuine in the beginning.
We were real.
But then something happened.
Life?
I can't blame life.
We happened.
Or didn't happen.
We didn't grow.
We didn't stay checked in with each other or our marriage.
Like two balloons let go together in the sky.
Even if they are tied together, eventually the tie comes undone. Eventually they drift apart.
I know I can't hold you responsible for my life.
I know that.
It's like therapist-talk 101.
But married people do affect one another.
They do influence and determine and change the course of each other's lives.
It's up to me to change my life back to the direction I always wanted it to go.

*Every individual has a place to fill in the world and is important in some respect whether he chooses to be so or not.*

*- Nathaniel Hawthorne*

*Every part of the journey is of importance to the whole.*

*- Teresa of Avila*

February 22, 2109

Dear J.,

Tonight at the end of yoga I began to cry.

Tears slipping ever so slowly down the side of my face as I laid there in the final pose of the night's efforts.

But the tears weren't for you.

They were for my mother.

I miss her so profoundly.

I guess yoga's combination of movement and music opens you emotionally as well as physically. Grief and rawness making their way to the surface.

It's not the first time I cried during yoga.

But it was the first time I thought of you.

I thought of how little you know about me.

I thought about how little you are aware of who I am.

I thought about how you don't even know I cry during yoga.

And how I would never tell you.

We don't even have the platform for me to tell you if I wanted to.

What would I do? Walk in and say,

"So, I cried tonight during yoga."

What would you say?

Probably nothing.

You'd just look at me.

Your silence speaking louder than any words.

I want you to know me.

Or should I say, I *wanted* you to know me?

How could you know me now?

How – where – would I even begin?

To fill you in.

To catch you up.

I am growing.

I know this.

I don't always feel this when I am home.

(Or should I say, I *never* feel this when I am home?)

When I am with you.

But when I am out in the world.

When I am interacting with other people.

The strength is coming back.

Who I am with you, around the kids sometimes too, I hate so much.

I am the *worse* version of myself with my family.

How tragic.

It makes my stomach churn to even write that.

But in the world, I get glimpses of Me.

The Me I want to be; the Me I know I can be; the Me I must be.

I will chase her til I catch her.

*I dwell in possibility.*

- *Emily Dickinson*

February 24, 2019

Dear J.,

Why do I keep forgetting how broken you are?
How can I forget how toxic and cruel you can be?
I go out of town for one night and our daughter in calling me crying because you are yelling for "no reason" and in a "really bad mood" and she doesn't "know why." But then she begs me – BEGS! ME! - not to call you because when I do, the furry you unleash on her is crushing. Sometimes I just hate you.
Sometimes you are such a fucking bastard!

*Do not look for healing at the feet of those who broke you.*

*- Rupi Kaur*

February 25, 2019

Dear J.,

    Know this:
    At this very moment, I hate you!
    Sitting in the basement.
    Playing those god damn fucking video games!
    I hate you for you ability to be completely self-absorbed.
    I hate you for your willingness to accept this fate for our marriage.
    I hate you for not being a man who participates in his marriage and loves his wife.
    I hate you for so many things you do and so many things you don't do.
    I hate you for who you are and I hate you for who you are not.
    But most of all, I hate you for who I feel myself becoming with you.

*Love is a very complicated path because on that path, things conspire to either raise us up to heaven or cast us down into hell.*

*- Paulo Coelho, By The River Piedra I Sat Down and Wept*

March 2, 2019

Dear J.,

Well tonight you actually did it.
Finally?
After all these years, after all the hateful, vile things you have said to me. Vicious, ugly things. Disturbing things no husband should ever say to his wife.
Fuck you.
Shut the fuck up.
Lick me.
I can't wait for you to die.
I fucking hate you.
These cruel, cruel, nasty, ugly, ugly things.
And yet, somehow I remained stuck.
Somehow I couldn't, wouldn't commit myself 100% to leaving you.
And then tonight.
Tonight you said something – the one thing I didn't even know there was for you to say – that has freed me.
You said,
"I don't trust you as far as I can spit."
You don't trust ME?!!
You?!!
Don't trust?!!
ME?!!!
You, who has verbally assaulted me. Embarrassed me and humiliated me. You, who has emotionally and mentally abandoned our marriage. You, who makes me feel bad about spending money at Starbucks, for wanting a new (expensive!) sewing machine. You who once scoffed at buying me a pair of hiking boots because they were

$100. You who treats me like a combination of maid/nanny/verbal punching bag.

Does not trust ME?!!!

How dare you!

How dare you question my morality.

My integrity.

My value as a human being.

How.

Dare.

You!

And yet you have set me free.

I am finally free.

Of hope.

Of responsibility.

Of guilt.

I.

Am.

Free.

How strange it seems.

That this transgression of yours, this declaration of mistrust, should be the straw that breaks my donkey-back.

Not all those straws of cruel, ugly words.

No.

That load I seemed to carry "just fine."

I'm sure a psychologist could explain why though I don't really understand it myself.

*Accept with wisdom the fact that the Path is full of contradictions.*

*- Paulo Coelho, The Spy*

March 3, 2019

Dear J.,

I can't stop thinking about what you said to me.
In all honesty, I am shocked at how deeply it hurt me.
I've been asking myself,
"Why?"
Why would I be so affected by those words of yours when you have said so many ugly – even uglier – words to me in the past?
And then I realized…
While all the things you have screamed, shouted and hissed at me were undoubtedly ugly and vicious and toxic, they were really all about you. Your anger, self-loathing and pain projected onto me.
"Fuck you."
"I hope you die."
Even you're go-to, "you're a fucking bitch" was never about me.
That was all, always, about you.
But when you said what you said…
That was about what you think of me as a person.
"I don't trust you as far as I can spit," says you think I am the lowest of human beings. It says you believe me to be a liar and a deceiver. A woman void of morals or ethics.
THAT'S why it both haunts me and sets me free.
How did you come to think so little of me?
Why would I continue to be with anyone who thinks so little of me?

*You can have a pet zebra and put that zebra into a small cage and everyday tell it the zebra that you love it, but no matter how the zebra and you love each other, the fact remains, that the zebra should be let out of that cage and should belong to someone who can treat it better, the way it should be treated, someone who can make it happy.*

*- C. JoyBell C.*

March 4, 2019

Dear J.,

You are a mean and cruel man.

I know you are also a lost, suffering man but that can no longer be my concern. You project your anger, your self-loathing, your life-long regrets and your family-history onto me.

These are bones that are buried deep within you.

Too deep.

For me to excavate.

For you to try to unearth.

Is it you can't?

Or you won't?

Does it matter?

The end result is the same.

For you.

But not for me.

Not anymore.

I am done.

I will be free.

*Toxic people attach themselves like cinder blocks around your ankles, and then invite you to swim in their own poisoned waters.*

*- John Markgreen*

March 5, 2019

Dear J.,

I have been thinking about what we have been fighting about.

We're fighting because I want you to go on a trip-of-a-life-time with the kids and me to Europe.

Do you see the absurdity in that?

Do you recognize the irony?

The foolishness?

The tragedy?

We're fighting basically because you won't allow yourself to dream. We're fighting because you want to arrest my dreaming.

We're fighting because I want more for us – for you – than you want for us or yourself.

I am not perfect.

But I am a dreamer.

I believe in life.

I love life.

I want to dream crazy dreams, pursue crazy ideas.

We're fighting because your only answer to everything (e-v-e-r-y-t-h-i-n-g!!)is,

"We don't have money for that!"

Any dream, any wish, any fantastical idea – no matter how big or small, no matter how imminent or far off in the future – you instantly kill it with,

"THERE'S NO MONEY!"

I am so very, very tired of hearing that!

I am so tired of being defeated before I even begin.

You live in a world of scarcity.

You live from a place of scarcity.

There will never be enough, in your mind.
Worse, you believe there *can't* ever be enough.
I know the Universe is an abundant entity.
A generous entity.
I am joining forces with it.
I welcome all the abundance it has to send my way.
Emotional, spiritual…
Financial.
The Universe is not Ebeneezer Scrooge.

The Universe is Santa Claus, the Tooth Fairy, your rich grandma and the multi-million dollar winning lottery ticket.

All rolled up into this fantastical energy called Life that IS available to me!!

*Focus on lack, and you will always struggle to create enough money. Your mind can grasp intellectual ideas, but it is in the FEELING that transformation takes place.*

*- Stephen Richards, Ask and the Universe Will Provide: A Straightforward Guide To Manifesting Your Dreams*

March 9, 2019

Dear J.,

It seems I keep writing this over and over again.

I don't think you will ever know or admit to yourself how so, so hard it is for me to leave you.

It is hard.

So very hard.

So very hard that it consumes my emotions during much of this letter-writing practice.

My heart aches for many reasons.

You couldn't withdraw yourself from me, our marriage and our life anymore while still physically being present if you tried, I dare say.

You are just so gone.

It's so hard for me to get my head around this.

How do you share a house (supposedly a life) with people you never really engage, never really talk to, never really take the time to know? How do you watch your kids grow up before you eyes without participating? Yes, you do the requisite sports games and practices. You will drive kids here or there if I ask you. If you haven't already taken "your turn." You will attend the special events, celebrate the milestones and yes, go on vacations though those often don't go so well but you go. But that's it. You do the minimum. The "required" but otherwise, you hold yourself separate from us, your family.

No Sunday trips to the zoo.

No fishing adventures.

No spontaneous jaunts for ice cream.

No walks through the neighborhood.

You won't even go to the fireworks on 4th of July anymore.

So what is there for me to do?

I go from being angry and resentful toward you to feeling bad for you, worrying about you.

But I am finally realizing my decision to leave you has nothing to do with how I feel about you. In fact, my decision *can't* have anything to do with how I feel about you. My decision is, and has to be, based on how I feel about me – with you and in this marriage.

And these days, I'm not feeling very good.

*Love yourself first and everything falls into line.*

*- Lucille Ball*

March 12, 2019

Dear J.,

I want to hate you right now.
I want to hate you so much.
I want to fill my being with an anger and disdain for you that knows no bounds.
But I know I shouldn't.
I can't.
I won't.
Because to hate you is to poison myself. To hate you is to create in myself an energy that is toxic and limiting. To hate you is to vibrate in the metaphysical realm on a level that is oppressive and destructive. To hate you is to create hatred within myself. To hate you is to destroy my life.
To hate you is to commit emotional, mental and spiritual suicide.
So I will strive to be grateful and forgiving.
I will be grateful for the pain you have brought into my life. I will see it as the pressure my life's chunk of coal needed to become the diamond it was meant to be. I will think of our children and the joy there was, the love there was, the laughter there was and teach myself to remember you with fondness. I will foster gratitude within myself for this challenge because out of this challenge, I can create greater things for myself. My life.
I will see the brokenness in our marriage as a gift.
I will see the anger and hatred you spew at me as a catalyst for my own great change.
I want to hate you but I won't.
Instead, I will love myself.
My life.

*The struggle ends when gratitude begins.*

*- Neale Donald Walsch*

March 13, 2019

Dear J.,

Today I got a new "bonus card" account at the grocery store.

I know that sounds like nothing. Trivial. Mundane, silly and irrelevant but it was actually a big step. Whenever I didn't have my card with me, I had to put in the phone number to get my rewards. Our phone number. The house phone number that you had before we married. The house phone number for a house that will soon not be my home.

I didn't want to continue to use that number.

Call it a metaphysical thing.

I didn't want to "confirm" that is my house, my phone number.

I know if I told you this, tried to explain it to you, you would laugh or shrug off the significance. Maybe belittle my effort or say something cynical like,

"Oh, right. That's certainly going to get you the money to buy your own house. Changing your grocery account."

But it's not about literally getting the money.

It's about energy.

I could feel the shift in my energy the minute I got my new card.

I felt a bit of trepidation.

"I'm really doing this," came a voice in my head.

The cord that binds us is made of many, many tiny strands.

Snipping even just one is a step forward.

An announcement to myself and the Universe that says,

"I am ready."

*The universe has no restrictions. You place restrictions on the universe with your expectations.*

*- Deepak Chopra*

March 15, 2019

Dear J.,

    I'm trying not to hate you.
    I'm trying not to resent you.
    I'm trying not to hold onto the bitterness and anger I feel toward you, the way you have treated me, what you have done to our marriage.
    I'm trying to let it all go.
    I know I have to let it all go.
    So what is the problem?
    Just you.
    Us.
    Being near one another.
    Having to still interact with one another.
    You stood up in my face and hissed,
    "I fucking HATE YOU!"
    How do I "let that go?"
    How do I process that?
    The magnitude of that. How can I even ever fully process the reality and ramifications of being married to a man who says such things to me?
    I know how you speak to me is "about you," not me.
    I know it is my responsibility not to give you power over me. Over my life.
    But when your husband screams,
    "I fucking HATE YOU!"
    It's hard to wrestle your power back from that.

*When we get comfortable with our own strength, discomfort changes shape. We remember our power.*

*- Jen Knox, The Glass City*

March 16, 2019

Dear J.,

It's the resentment I can't seem to let go of.

The resentment over the complete and utter disregard you have for what I bring to the family and the household. Resentment over the fact that you see no value in what I do as the mother of our children.

Your words over the years…

Your uber-control of the (household!) finances…

Your lack of actions…

All this says to me that you see me as little more than a drain on YOUR money. Your actions tell me that you believe because I don't contribute equally in financial terms to our finances that I am not equal to you.

Every time I am working my ass off for a kid's birthday party or driving kids 100 different directions or up til 1 am preparing whatever it is someone needs for the next day, I think of how you feel I "do nothing.

There is so many things to mourn in the end of a marriage.

And for me, one of those things is knowing that you have shown such little respect for me in the role of mother to our children. Even more painful, you have never taught our children respect for my role as their mother.

It is important to note that research has shown that men who have abusive mothers do not tend to develop especially negative attitudes toward females, but men who have abusive fathers do; the disrespect that abusive men show their wives and their daughters is often absorbed by their sons.

*- Lundy Bancroft, Why Does He Do That? Inside the Minds of Angry and Controlling Men*

I think maybe, when I was young, I witnessed a chaste kiss between the two when it was impossible to avoid. Christmas, birthdays. Dry lips. On their best married days, their communications were entirely transactional: 'We're out of milk again.' (I'll get some today.) 'I need this ironed properly.' (I'll do that today.) 'How hard is it to buy milk?' (Silence.) 'You forgot to call the plumber.' (Sigh.) Goddammit, put on your coat, right now, and go out and get some goddam milk. Now.' These messages and orders brought to you by my father, a mid-level phone company manager who treated my mother at best like an incompetent employee.

*- Gillian Flynn, Gone Girl*

April 2, 2019

Dear J.,

If there is one thing I wish I could make you understand – appreciate even – it would be the profound – PRO-FOUND!! - depth of despair your verbal abuse and outbursts create within me. I don't know if I can even remotely begin to explain the jarring affect your language has on the house, my soul…
Our children.
To say it "cuts to the quick" would certainly be the understatement of the century. You're not around you. You experience you from the inside. What you language does to you, I don't know. But I will tell you, as the people on the outside of you, hearing you continually cursing "god damn" this and "fuck" that, it is draining.
It leaches the very life from our souls.

*The words with which a child's heart is poisoned, whether through malice or through ignorance, remain branded in his memory, and sooner or later they burn his soul.*

*- Carlos Ruiz Zafon, The Shadow of the Wind*

April 12, 2019

Dear J.,

Even as I become more and more resigned to leaving you…

Even as I become more and more excited about my new life…

Your words, your moods, your toxic language and general hostility toward life affects me.

I try.

I try to disconnect myself from your words, your moods, your energy.

I try to live from a place of kindness, patience and joy.

I'm not very good at it, I'm afraid.

I read how Nelson Mandela extended love, understanding and forgiveness to the guards that guarded – and beat – him for his 30+ years imprisoned.

I know this isn't prison and good thing because I am no Nelson Mandela. If only I could extent a tiny fraction of the grace he was able to offer in a far more horrific situation, I suppose I would do well. If only I could live from a place of peace while residing in an emotional war zone. If only I could do as all the gurus and writers and wise ones say and not allow your actions to affect my being.

If only…

I were stronger, better, more of what I need to be.

*Work hard for what you want because it won't come to you without a fight. You have to be strong and courageous and know you can do anything you put your mind to. If somebody puts your down or criticizes you, just keep on believing in yourself and turn it into a positive.*

- Leah LaBelle

*You have to be strong and calm to overcome difficult moments.*

*- Dani Alves*

April 20, 2019

Dear J.,

It is Saturday night, 8:00 pm.
Tomorrow is Easter.
I am sitting in my car, having just left the grocery store.
We have no plans as a family for Easter.
But of course, I will create the Easter baskets.
I will go to church with our daughter.
I will cook dinner.
A ham.
Even though I don't even eat ham.
And I will clean up from it.
I will patch together some sort of Easter celebration.
You?
You're on your way to being drunk tonight.
I just feel such desperation to be free from this situation.
To be free from our marriage.
To be free, I'm so very sorry to say, from you.

*Love never dies a natural death.*
*It dies because we don't know how to replenish its source.*
*It dies of blindness and errors and betrayals.*
*It dies of illness and wounds; it dies of weariness, of withering, of tarnishing.*

*- Anais Nin*

April 26, 2019

Dear J.,

You know, I fantasize about him.

The man who would love me.

The man who would look lovingly into my eyes.

The man who would find me beautiful and wonderful and who would smile with adoration at my quirks and idiosyncrasies.

The man who would make me feel valued and cherished and adored.

And it is when I think about this imaginary man, when I imagine the feelings I would feel at being loved, that I recognize how much our empty marriage has broken me.

I don't mean to be dumping on you but do you really grasp the affects on a woman when she is married to a man who ignores her? Doesn't kiss her good-night as they lay down at night or good-morning when he leaves for work? Doesn't call her during the day, check in with her for "no reason" or acknowledge who she is.

I used to (USED! TO!) wake up every morning and my very first thought was,

"He left again without kissing me good-bye."

My..

Very…

FIRST!

Thought.

I used to ask you why you don't kiss me good-bye, tell you how important it was to me. You'd say something like you "didn't want to wake me up."

I don't even know what that bullshit answer is suppose to mean or justify.

But it's ok.
I'm used to it now.
Don't even think about it any more in the morning.
It is what it is, as the saying go.
And yet, I doubt I am really "used to it."
Not completely.
On some level, I am sure (afraid) the emptiness, the vacancy, the loveless-ness in our marriage is affecting me.
I want to be free of this pain.
Of being alone but not alone.
Of lying next to someone who is there but not present.

Sometimes when I go to bed at night, I pretend I am alone in my own bed in my own house, nothing but dogs and cats sleeping next to me. It feels wonderful. Peaceful. Tranquil. To be alone with one's own company is not lonely. It's not the nothingness of being alone while with someone. To be alone with just your own company can be quite delightful.

But to be alone while with someone is quite dreadful.

*I used to think the worse thing in life was to end up all alone, it's not. The worse thing in life is to end up with people who make you feel alone.*

*- Robin Williams*

April 27, 2019

Dear J.,

No longer do I waver or oscillate in my need to leave you.
I will be 60 years old next year.
60!
Years!
Old!!
As someone said to me,
"That's not old but it's not young either."
The truth is I can't wait – CAN'T! WAIT! - to sleep in my own bed! To feel an unspoken truth, rather than an unspoken tension, as I close my eyes at night. I am comfortable, happy, excited about my decision. About my new life that awaits me.
But that doesn't mean you don't still affect me with your words, your moods, your anger.
I wish you didn't.
I wish none of what you say or do affected me.
Made its way into my soul.
But it does.
Clearing myself of your toxicity while we still live together is like shoveling the driveway while it's still snowing. I'm never going to be completely free of you until I am completely free of you.
I don't know if I will be sad about finally being gone when the day comes. I've been sad about us for such a very long time that perhaps my grieving will be complete by the time I leave.
Part of me will always be sorry, I suspect.
Not sorry I left.
Sorry we were another causality.
Another divorce.

Our marriage another statistic.

I never wanted *to be* divorced but what choice is there?

*Why do they not teach you that time is a finger-snap and an eye-blink, and that you should not allow a moment to pass you by without taking joyous, ecstatic note of it, not wasting a single moment of its swift, breakneck circuit?*

*- Pat Conroy*

April 29, 2019

Dear J.,

Tonight you were in a foul mood.

That's not really anything so unusual but usually I have an idea of where you anger is coming from or there is some indication as to the reason for your bad mood. Tonight there seemed to be no obvious reason. None that I could recognize anyway and so I asked you,

"Why are you in such a bad mood?"

You hissed at me, that all-too familiar hatred in your eyes,

"Leave me alone!"

"What is going on with you?" I dared.

"Just leave me alone!" You hissed again. "I'm having one of the worse anxiety attacks ever."

I was shocked!

Would seem nothing could shock me after our years together and all the things you have said to me but yes, I was shocked.

And saddened.

In the more than 20 years we have been together – whether dating or married - you have never, ever, EVER ONCE identified your hostility or anger as anxiety. You have never, ever, EVER told me you were having an anxiety attack!

How could I not know this?

How could it be that this has never been said between us?

Is it my fault?

Should I have somehow recognized your outbursts for the anxiety they may have been? At least some of the time?

But how could I, would I have known?

If you have never once labeled it for me?

If I think the animal that wandered into my house is a cat and

I'm always remarking on how stinky it is, is it my fault for not knowing it's a skunk? If no one ever told me? Of course it stinks. It's a skunk. But I thought it was a cat all along.

I don't know what I thought your anger, your verbal assaults, your hostility "was." Just anger, I suppose. How could I recognize it as a by-product of anxiety if you never, ever, EVER once identified it for me?

I left you alone, per your request but I wanted to say,

"All these years. We could have been working through this. I could have been there for you. We could have been a team. *I could have helped you!*"

Yes, I could have helped.

I don't know how.

Not now.

Not in retrospect.

Not now that it is too late.

But you could have leaned on me, your wife. We could have taken this beast on together. We could have grown together. Learned together. What we needed from each other. What we needed from ourselves. I could have been there to offer comfort, safety, an escape from the world.

*We could have been a team.*

If you had trusted me.

If you had let me.

Maybe it's not so much you've been withdrawing the past few years.

Maybe it's just I'm finally noticing.

How removed you've always been.

*The best thing to hold onto in life is each other.*

*- Audrey Hepburn*

April 30, 2019

Dear J.,

Oh my!
Oh my, oh my, OH!! MY!!
I will love you!
Yes.
I.
Will.
Love you!
I'm not staying with you. (And I'm not drunk.)
I haven't changed my desire to create a new life for myself – my own life – a life that you, sadly, are no longer a part of.
But I will love you.
I have started listening to this woman who goes by the name of Abraham Hicks. She talks about our inner beings and our vortexes and all the Universe is holding for us, if we'd just take the time to align ourselves with the energy of the Universe. You know, all the stuff you think I am crazy to believe in.
She said we must love even those who seem unlovable.
But more importantly, she says our inner being, our spiritual or divine being *already does love those who seem unlovable!*
However, our outer being, our Earthly being, is the entity that struggles. That has to catch up with the love our inner being feels for all.
I've been re-reading these letters.
I was going to read "them all" one night and yet I got through only a few. Then I couldn't bring myself to read any more for several days. I was surprised. Wondered why. Nothing about what I was reading was new to me. After all, I wrote it. Lived it.

It seemed reading my own words should be simple.

But now I understand why it is so taxing. So draining.

Because I am no longer in the same place I was as when I began writing these letters. I started over a year ago – the beginning of 2018. I was conflicted and torn and angry and hating and confused.

I wanted to leave.

I didn't want to leave.

I was hating you.

I was feeling bad for you.

I saw you as a full-blown asshole.

I saw you as someone in pain and suffering.

It was all there – the whole gamete of human emotions.

But I have moved through them!

I have!

And so now, as Abraham Hicks says, I am ready to be ready.

First, she says, you are getting ready to be ready to be ready to be ready.

But if you keep moving, you keep working at it, you keep seeking the truth, one day you are...

Ready to be ready.

I am ready to be ready to vibrate on a higher level.

I am ready to be ready to leave the anger and hatred behind.

I will leave you.

I will lose you.

I will let go of all I thought my marriage would be, my life would be, when I married you.

But I will also love you.

*One ends a romantic relationship while remaining a compassionate friend, by being kind above all else. By explaining one's decision to leave the relationship with love and respect and emotional transparency.*

*By being honest without being brutal. By expressing gratitude for what was given. By taking responsibilities for mistakes and attempting to make amends. By acknowledging that one's decision has caused another to suffer. By suffering because of that. By having the guts to stand by one's partner even while one is leaving. By talking it all the way through and by listening. By honoring what once was. By bearing witness to the undoing and salvaging what one can. By being a friend, even if an actual friendship is impossible.*

*- Cheryl Strayed, Brave Enough*

May 3, 2019

Dear J,.

It's not going to be so easy, this loving you thing, is it?
Tonight we got in a huge argument over the $175 Verizon bill.
Who would pay it.
A toxic, soul sucking argument over $175.
Why do I let myself get sucked into your pain?
Why do I let myself be diminished by your fears?
You live from a place a scarcity.
Joy, happiness…money. All scarce and insufficient in quantity.
I am so angry with myself for allowing myself to be sucked into your world.
I won't live in your world any longer.
I won't live small.
The world is too grand.
The potential for our journeys too great.

*I understand the logic behind removing toxic people from one's life. But I also understand many who are "toxic" are acting out of a painful past…and that to marginalize someone who's not known much love is to validate that they don't matter. To live in the world we desire – a world of good people, safe places – requires less fence-building and more heart-building. It requires valuing the worth of all people and loving the hurt as much as possible.*

*- Renata Bowers*

May 9, 2019

Dear J.,

Today I was visiting with a friend.

Her father-in-law is 92 years old and just moved into a "facility." She said it is as nice as any "facility" can be but the other day her brother-in-law had to go over and "confiscate" all his underwear. Seems her father-in-law is not as good as getting to the toilet as he believes and things are stinking up a good deal in his room.

They "secretly" replaced all his underwear with "Depends."

How sad.

Life is not kind to the aging body.

As she was telling me of the situation, I had two thoughts.

One was, of course, dear God please let me die before this becomes my fate but the second was if, if I find myself to be in the place where my body fails me before my mind, I don't want to look back and feel that I lost even one minute of one day of my healthy days, my vibrant days, my days of limitless potential, to smallness, to self-imposed limitations, to baseless doubts or fears.

I just can't live the way we live any longer.

*Dwell on the beauty of life.*
*Watch the stars, and see yourself running with them.*

*- Marcus Aurelius*

*Stop acting so small. You are the universe in ecstatic motion.*

*- Rumi*

May 14, 2019

Dear J.,

I think this should be my last letter to you.

I started writing these letters to you as a way of processing my my feelings about leaving but also with the thought (hope?) that one day you would read them and maybe get some understanding of why I left. I wanted you to have an understanding of what my experience in our marriage was not so you could feel bad or wrong or guilty but so that you would know that leaving you was so very hard.

And that the decision was extremely long in the realization.

Perhaps most of all, I wanted you to know that ultimately it was not about hating you.

It was about wanting to love myself again.

It was about needing to love myself again.

But now, as I want to move forward, I realize that these letters have been more than a processing effort. More than a cathartic writing exercise. The letters, the writing, has taken on a life of its own. It's given me a connection to you where there was virtually none. Obviously a one-sided connection but still, a real connection for me nonetheless

And so, I think I need to sever this connection. The last connection? The only connection?

Perhaps.

But if I am going to finally disconnect from you physically, I need to disconnect from you emotionally and mentally.

But first I want, need, to make sure – one last time – that you really understand why I left.

It wasn't the verbal assaults – though it probably should have been.

It wasn't the damage I feared our marriage was doing to our children – though maybe it should have been.

It wasn't how absent and removed you were from our marriage – though probably another valid reason.

It wasn't even the loneliness and anger and longing of what was becoming, if it wasn't already was, a loveless marriage.

It wasn't any of the things that people always think it is when a marriage fails.

It was my awakening to how much life we – I – had let slip away in 19+ years of marriage.

We don't have a GATE to the backyard fence.

No gate.

Almost 20 years in our house and we have never managed to build a gate for the fence. Instead, we have these pieces of decorative fencing – that most certainly were never meant to contain big, rambunctious dogs - that we bungee cord together.

Which I guess hardly sounds horrible except every time I need to pass from the backyard to the front, I need to painstakingly un-bungee-cord the whole contraption.

And so yesterday, as I was going through the whole un-bungee/re-bungee cord process, I started getting SO MAD!

I mean it was a rage.

A deep, searing RAGE coming from the depths of my soul as I worked those god damn, stupid frayed bungee cords. It was crazy. I knew it myself yet I seemed unable to abate or mitigate it.

I yelled. Cursed. I wanted to punch the fucking crap out of something, anything.

And then it hit me:

The anger had nothing to do with the actual bungee/unbungee process.

But it did have *everything* to do with what the unbungee/bungee cord process represents!

And what it represents is all we have never done, not gotten around to or allowed into our lives in the past nearly 20 years (20! YEARS!!) of marriage. The unbungee/bungee process is all the dreams never dreamed, adventures never taken, plans never made, goals never reached. Heck, I don't think we ever even set a single goal for ourselves. Not as a family, not as a couple, not even as individuals. We just went from one day to the next without ever so much as a mumble between us of what we wanted for ourselves, our lives, our children.

Can I blame you entirely?

No, of course not.

But as my husband, your energy, your attitude, your willingness DID affect me. How could it not? You were like a pebble in my shoe that became a rock that became a boulder tethered to my ankle.

Is that too harsh?

Mean?

I can see how it would sound so.

Like all I am doing is blaming you for the unhappiness I am feeling now. Perhaps I am. Is that fair? Can I blame you that I haven't done more in my life, for my life, in the past 19 years that we've been married?

I know any therapist would say that I can't "blame" you or anyone else for my choices, my actions and decisions but life does have cause and affect. And frankly, over the past 19+ years, our marriage has caused me to make choices that now has affected my life in a way that is troubling. Disappointing. Overwhelming.

And so that is why I am finally leaving.

Not because of the verbal abuse.

Not because you are distant and removed from our marriage and me.

Not for the kids even.

I'm leaving because it's leave now or lose more of my life later.
I'm sorry.
I truly am.
I wish it had all been so very different.
Good-bye.

*Hope is the thing with feathers*
*That perches in your soul*
*And sings the tune without words*
*And never stops at all.*

*- Emily Dickenson*

May 16, 2019

Dear J.,

I thought I was done writing you.
I thought I had said all I needed to say, could say, there was to say.
Then this week-end.
Another blow-up between us.
And I was reminded.
I do blame you for the end of our marriage.
I do see it as your fault we failed.
However, this is not the same thing as saying you were the only one who was ever wrong.
No, no, I am not saying that.
I have no doubt there were ways I could have changed, been better, understood your needs more.
So no, you weren't all wrong, all the time.
But the failure of our marriage is your fault.
Because you would not work to save us.
You would not do the internal work for yourself.
You would not do the work together for us.
You would not do the work our family needed.
So yes, I blame you.
And yet, I have to let that blame go.
I have to let it all go.
The blame.
Our marriage.
You.
My expectations of what my family would be.
And the future.

Most of all I have to let go of the future I envisioned.
So I can build a future that will be…
All I've always wanted for my life.

*There is no satisfaction that can compare with looking back across the years and finding you've grown in self-control, judgment, generosity and unselfishness.*

*- Ella Wheeler Wilcox*

May 23, 2019

Dear J.,

I keep thinking I need to write one more letter.
That I need to explain one more time.
That I can explain one more time.
That I need to make myself clear one last time.
But I'm wrong.
There's nothing left to say.
Really.
I have expressed my anger, my grief, my resentment, my sadness.
I have written words of condemnation but also of forgiveness.
I've told you of my regrets but hopefully also of my gratitude.

I've spelled out, maybe too well, the pain and longing of losing what I thought my life, our marriage, our future together would have been.

But hopefully, somewhere in there, I have expressed an appreciation for what we did have.

A fondness for the joy and laughter there was…
A tenderness for love we did share…
If not forever…
At least for awhile.

*Don't you ever say I just walked away.*

*- Miley Cyrus, Wrecking Ball*

# CONTACT

Thank you for sharing in my story and journey.

Should you feel the desire, my email is:
WrenRWaters@gmail.com

Made in the USA
Las Vegas, NV
30 January 2022